D1246597

BOWEN THEORY & PRACTICE

Georgetown Family Center
Washington, DC

Also published by the Georgetown Family Center

Understanding Organizations

The Emotional Side of Organizations

Family Systems: A Journal of Natural Systems
Thinking in Psychiatry and the Sciences

BOWEN THEORY & PRACTICE

FEATURE ARTICLES FROM THE
FAMILY CENTER REPORT
1979-1996

EDITED BY
RUTH RILEY SAGAR

Georgetown Family Center
4400 MacArthur Boulevard, NW, Suite 103
Washington, DC 20007-2521

Editor: Ruth Riley Sagar
Design and Production: Elizabeth M. Utschig

Printed on acid-free paper.

ISBN 0-9658540-0-0

Library of Congress Catalogue Card Number: 97-65744

Printed in the United States of America

ACKNOWLEDGEMENTS

Special acknowledgement for the publication of this book is extended to Dr. Murray Bowen whose observations and ideas led to the development of family systems theory, upon which all the papers in this collection are based; to Dr. Michael Kerr whose work in extending theory is reflected in the many articles he has published here; and to the faculty of the Georgetown Family Center, past and present, who wrote the feature articles selected for this collection and who also wrote extensively about the academic, clinical, and research activities they developed over the last eighteen years.

I would like to thank Elizabeth Utschig whose design of the book so well captures the elements of the original publication and also reflects the union of theory and practice which has been the hallmark of the Georgetown Family Center, and Marjorie Hottel who handled distribution of the Family Center Report since the first issue was published in 1979. A special thank you also goes to Scott Meyer who first saw the importance of publishing a formal, periodic account of Family Center activities as the family program at Georgetown University neared its twentieth anniversary.

Finally, I would like to express my admiration of the contributors whose endeavors have led to increased knowledge about the human as an adapting, evolving part of all life.

R.R.S.

PREFACE

The Georgetown Family Center began publishing the *Family Center Report* in January 1979 amid a period of rapid development of training programs, clinical services, and research ideas based on family systems theory. Twenty years of experience in developing and refining theory had put Georgetown in a position of prominence in the field, and an increasing number of professionals from around the country were seeking knowledge about systems theory and therapy.

In 1979 Dr. Bowen's book, *Family Therapy in Clinical Practice,* had just been published, and the faculty had initiated its most ambitious academic year to date. In addition to the Annual Symposium, then in its nineteenth year, the Family Center brought together for the Human Family Symposium fifty leaders from family therapy, psychiatry, and the social and biological sciences who had been influential in developing the field of family theory and therapy. Smaller, specialized symposia on juvenile delinquency, on the biological and emotional aspects of cancer, on family theory and nursing practice, on biofeedback, on aging, and on the application of family systems theory to work organizations were on the calendar for the upcoming year.

The *Family Center Report* was envisioned as a way not only to review events but also as a forum for presenting ideas and research in progress. Papers on such subjects as natural selection theory, the family as an emotional unit, population density, as well as a systems model for disease, family diagnosis, and emotional process in society served as feature articles.

Perhaps the most historically significant article to appear in the
Report is Dr. Bowen's "Subjectivity, Homo Sapiens and Science,"
written in the fall of 1982. In this paper he makes explicit his
view that human behavior could become a science and that the
greatest barrier to achieving that goal is human subjectivity. He
recounts his own work in developing a scientific view of man
and what was involved in switching from "thinking mental health"
to "thinking science."

The ramification of making this goal a reality redefined the position of the Family Center in the field, and recalibrated the efforts
of individual faculty members to work on this goal in their own
way. Many of the feature articles that follow reflect these efforts.

The stimulus for publishing this collection came from reviewing
the inventory of back issues of the *Report*. The Family Center
decided to discontinue publishing the *Family Center Report* in
the summer of 1996. The journal, *Family Systems,* had been
launched two years earlier, and the energy and resources for writing have been concentrated there. During this process of decid-
ing how to preserve back issues for the archives, it became ap-
parent that there were many substantive, well-developed papers,
as relevant today as when they were first written. By publishing
them in one volume, the hope is to give them the wider exposure
they merit and to make them available for the future.

Ruth Riley Sagar

July 1997
Washington, DC

CONTENTS

=== Theory ===

x   ═══ Practice ═══════════════════

THEORY

PRACTICE

Significance of Murray Bowen's Scientific Contributions

Michael E. Kerr, MD

My task and privilege this afternoon is to address the significance of Dr. Murray Bowen's contributions to knowledge and to the human cause. While each of us here is aware that Dr. Bowen has already made important contributions, it will be the next several generations that determine the full extent of those contributions. What they learn will show how accurate an observer of nature Dr. Bowen has been.

This day was designed to honor Murray Bowen but, knowing him as I do, I believe that he would prefer that the focus not be on him but on the order that exists in the natural world. Bowen's "window" on the natural world has largely been the human family and human society. He has always regarded the particular window he has looked through as one of many possible vantage points—all interesting and exciting—from which to view nature. When Bowen looked at the family, he assumed that he was looking at the natural world. When Bowen saw orderly and predictable patterns in the human family, he assumed that the order was somehow related to an order that existed in all nature.

It is almost glib to refer to "the order in the natural world." It sounds impressive, but what does it really mean? Is it a philosophy about the nature of things? Is there a scientific basis for thinking of nature as orderly, as conforming to particular laws

Published in Volume 7, No. 4, Fall 1986.

This paper was first a presentation made October 19, 1986 at the University of Tennessee—Knoxville as part of the State of Tennessee and University of Tennessee's recognition of Dr. Murray Bowen for Homecoming '86.

and patterns? Are the concepts we create that ascribe an order to nature strictly figments of our imagination?

In 1938 Albert Einstein wrote the following:

> Physical concepts are free creations of the human mind, and are not, however it may seem, uniquely determined by the external world. In our endeavor to understand reality we are somewhat like a man trying to understand the mechanism of a closed watch. He sees the face and the moving hands, even hears its ticking, but he has no way of opening the case. If he is ingenious he may form some picture of a mechanism which could be responsible for all the things he observes, but he may never be quite sure his picture is the only one which could explain his observations. He will never be able to compare his picture with the real mechanism and he cannot even imagine the possibility of the meaning of such a comparison.[1]

Einstein's metaphor is about scientific theory. Knowledge about nature accumulates through the ages. Each century more is learned about the predictability of the movements of the watch's hands and about the sounds and regularity of its ticks. Scientific concepts and theories are the "picture" our mind forms of the mechanisms that may account for what is observed. These concepts are not equivalent to nature and they are only as valid as they are consistent with what has been observed.

We encounter several obstacles when trying to develop a new theory or to extend an existing theory so that it will better explain the phenomena of our experiences. An obvious and important obstacle is the limits technology places on the movements that can be seen and the ticks that can be heard. As technology advances, we see and hear more. A second and perhaps more

---

[1] Albert Einstein and Leopold Infeld. 1938. *The Evolution of Physics*. New York: Simon and Schuster, p. 31.

important obstacle to advancing theory is, oddly enough, presently accepted theory. Accepted theory becomes an obstacle when our mind's picture of nature becomes equated with nature itself. When this happens, the human's view of nature is impeded; the window is fogged up. This means that observations inconsistent with our mind's picture are either not seen, or they are ignored, or they are molded so as to no longer appear inconsistent. Perhaps we do not see anything new because we are too busy watching the picture that supports the view of nature we already have. We can ignore inconsistent data by calling it "unimportant" or asserting that it reflects faulty data collection. We can shape observations more to our liking by embellishing them with a tinge of imagination and subjectivity.

Theory can be advanced when it is not equated with nature itself. This keeps it flexible and open to being changed by the observation of new movements and new sounds. In other words, our mind's picture does not screen out or shape observations; the observations are used to shape our mind's picture. So while our mind's picture can never be equated with nature itself, the picture can gradually be honed to be more and more consistent with what has been observed.

In time, a theory can come to be regarded as scientific fact. This does not occur on a specific day or in a specific year. One observation or some dramatic development usually does not convert a theory into fact. It is a matter of many observations accumulating, none of which are inconsistent with the theory. For example, evolution is either very close to being or now is regarded as a fact. While many of the details and mechanisms of evolution are still debated, evolution itself is probably no longer a theory. In contrast, psychoanalytic theory is still a theory; it is not accepted as fact. Bowen's family systems theory is a theory. The accumulation of data by present and future generations will determine if it becomes a passé theory or a scientific fact.

Each of us has our pictures of the nature of human behavior and human problems. Our pictures are strongly influenced by the pictures held and espoused by those around us. Most of us are careless about discerning where our picture begins and nature leaves off. Much of the time it may not be important to distinguish between our picture of the external world and the external world itself. Much of the business of daily life can be conducted without thinking very much about it. The progress of science, however, totally depends on thinking about it. Scientific training, while effective in teaching the methods of science, does not guarantee that one will not equate one's picture of the world with the world itself. Scientists can be just as guilty of ignoring and molding observations as anyone else.

Charles Darwin was one scientist who had little formal training in his field before he developed his theory of evolution. He said that he was fortunate to have been so poorly trained before embarking on his five-year voyage on the H.M.S. Beagle because it may have enabled him to see more than he was "supposed" to see. Perhaps because Darwin's picture of the natural world was inadequately formed or perhaps because Darwin was just Darwin, he was stimulated by his observations of nature to develop a coherent theory that others had only guessed at. Had Darwin increased rather than decreased our distortions about the way nature is organized, most of us probably would not have heard of him. Nature made Darwin famous.

What are these people like who can see more than they were trained to see? Have they been inadequately trained as Darwin suggested? Do they never lose sight of the fact that their picture of the natural world, and others' pictures of the natural world, are not equivalent to nature? Do they suffer from some kind of "mind itch" that will not allow them to put puzzles down until they are convinced they have done the best they could with them, at least for now? Are they ignorant people who know they are ignorant? Do they have a healthy mistrust of what they already think?

Linus Pauling's mind has itched for a long time. Several years ago I had the good fortune of hearing him speak. He described what he went through in coming up with the structure of hemoglobin. He called his type of research "theoretical medicine" and described it as follows:

> If you want to get results in almost any field of research, I believe that you have to devote yourself, your whole effort, to thinking about it. When you are lying in bed, when you are walking, or when you are on a bus. I start to think about a problem, and work at it at any desk with a calculator or computer. I work away perhaps for a week, for many weeks, until I am not getting anywhere. Then night after night, I lie in bed waiting to go to sleep, looking at this problem, thinking about it. Then later, perhaps even years later, I would suddenly have an idea and that was the solution to the problem. I had prepared my unconscious to examine everything that entered my mind with respect to that problem and finally something came along that I recognized as related to it. This is theoretical research. It is thinking about the problem until you think of something new that is pertinent to it. You can't expect to get anything new if you think about it five minutes a day. You have to think about it day and night.[2]

I have heard Murray Bowen say that he "dreamed" his theory. He went to sleep with a question and awoke with an answer. While this may not inspire confidence in the validity of his observations or concepts, I think he was talking about the same kind of thing Pauling described. Bowen never has been able to turn his head off.

---

[2] From a lecture delivered at Georgetown University, March 1980.

I think we can assume that Bowen was "adequately" trained. He did spend eight years at one of the country's premier psychiatric training institutions, the Menninger Clinic. So we cannot explain his ability to produce a genuinely new idea on the basis of his being trained inadequately to see what he was "supposed" to see. I think Bowen is one of those people who has an extraordinary ability to maintain a distinction between his picture of nature and nature itself. In addition, his mind itched. It still itches.

I started out today saying that I wanted to focus on nature, not on Bowen. Thus far I have not done that. I have focused on the way people like Bowen look at nature and have tried to guess at whatever it is that permits them to look at something that everybody else has looked at and see something that no one else has ever seen.

It is difficult to separate Bowen from the theory he developed because, in many ways, the theory is about the things that I have been talking about thus far. We humans are highly suggestible. We adopt our pictures of the world and its inhabitants from others, and our ability to observe rarely ever approaches what our nervous systems are capable of. Yet, we are not all the same in this regard. Bowen created a theory about this. It is a theory about the characteristics of a way of thinking that is fairly open to seeing the world more as it is, the characteristics of a way of thinking that is not open, and the characteristics of all graduations in between. The theory has several concepts about what influences this variation among people.

Darwin developed a plausible theory about the world not having been created as it then appeared, but a world which had undergone gradual changes over millions and millions of years. These changes occurred both in inanimate objects and animate forms. *Homo sapiens* is a product of these changes, whether we like it or not. The natural world is not constrained by what we wish or imagine it to be; only its inhabitants are constrained by wishes and fears of what might be. Darwin's theory established man's physical relationship to the subhuman forms. It is not a coincidence, in other words, that both men and monkeys have two arms and two legs. Darwin demonstrated a process by which similar outcomes could occur, the process of natural selection.

Man's behavioral link to the subhuman forms is another matter. Most of us have come to accept that human anatomy and physiology has been shaped by the same evolutionary processes that have shaped the anatomy and physiology of all living things, and that the scientific laws that apply to our anatomy and physiology probably apply throughout the animate world. But how do most of us think about human behavior? Is it not the tendency to make the human a special case? While we may often say that human beings act "like a bunch of animals," we think of man as mostly a cultured being. He has a brain, he talks, he thinks. He is different. Bowen has said—others have said—that most of our theories about human behavior are built on emphasizing the way the human is different from other animals. They emphasize the mind, psychological processes, and the newer portions of the human brain. Most theory builders have either not defined or emphasized what is naturally occurring behavior in man— behavior that is a product of man's evolutionary heritage.

Bowen did not ignore the influence of culture or the unique aspects of human psychology on behavior, but he did not lay the foundation stones for his theory on culture and psychology. He thought those sands shifted too quickly and in often unpredictable ways to trust anchoring a theory about man's behavior there. In addition, he was aware that when the discipline to compare one's picture of nature with nature itself is not enforced, imagination has free rein. Bowen wanted to build a theory, a picture, that would always be open to being reshaped by new or more careful observations of nature. As he is fond of saying, "When you get bogged down in a question about theory, go back to the rats. The rats don't lie." The rats, obviously, relate to processes much broader than human culture and psychology. The rats are one stone in the foundation.

Based on extensive reading, hours of thinking (and dreaming), and hours and hours and hours of listening to and watching the human family—along with constantly monitoring the ever compelling tendency to equate his existing picture of the world with the world itself—Bowen decided to lay the foundation stones of his theory on the evolutionary process and natural systems. Human behavior, while having many unique aspects, has been shaped by the same evolutionary processes that have shaped the behavior of all living things, and the scientific laws that apply to human behavior apply throughout the animate world. This is the assumption of family systems theory. This is why his program at Georgetown has reached out to all of the scientific disciplines. Every study of the natural world, whether it be in the genetics of fruit flies, the communication of whales, or the behavior of cancer cells, is relevant to the development of a science of human behavior. Man's anatomy, physiology, and behavior can be linked to all that is there to be seen in naturally occurring systems.

Bowen made a corollary assumption to man's being a part of nature—that the clinical dysfunctions are a product of that part of man he has in common with the lower forms. What we call "diseases" can be more adequately explained by viewing them as the outcome of a natural process. This assumption, which is not easy to think about, has far reaching implications. It is very easy to see a symptom; it can be very difficult to see the processes that lead up to a symptom.

What made it possible to conceptualize man's link to the natural world was the application of systems thinking. Systems thinking is really very simple. But because there are so many pieces to consider, it becomes very complex. Our minds tend to either retreat from complexity or beat on it until it is bludgeoned into "submission." We typically reduce complexity, not by seeing simple patterns, but by imposing simplistic explanations. Fortunately, there are people who can resist this temptation. People who can be comfortable with complexity long enough to begin to see simple patterns in it. Bowen did this with the human family. He did it with a very simple way of thinking that has existed for thousands of years. That way of thinking is seeing the natural world in terms of a continuous series of changes, each change being linked to the previous one. This way of thinking dissolves the compartments of knowledge, or at least has the potential to do so. It is a way of thinking that can permit one to engage complexity without beating on it or chopping it into pieces. It is a way of thinking that permits the inclusion of genes, brain cell receptors, hormones, psychology, the family, institutions, and society in the understanding of schizophrenia and cancer and whatever.

Process or systems thinking is very old. Darwin's theory describes a process. But as Carl Sagan points out, process thinking is very much older than the nineteenth century. As early as the sixth century BC, more than 2,500 years ago, the Greeks living in Ionia thought in terms of process. To quote Sagan's description of their accomplishments:

> Suddenly there were people who believed that everything was made of atoms; that human beings and other animals had sprung from simpler forms; that diseases were not caused by demons or the gods; that the Earth was only a planet going around the Sun. And that the stars were very far away.[3]

This way of thinking, although it did not disappear completely, was not influential for another 2,000 years when Copernicus, Galileo, Newton, and Darwin breathed new life into it.

---

[3] Carl Sagan. 1980. *Cosmos.* New York: Random House, p. 174.

People like Newton and Darwin could not get away with merely asserting that the motions of the planets were linked or that existing species were created by a gradual series of continuous changes. Others had said such things and had been dismissed. Newton and Darwin had to offer plausible concepts to account for these asserted interrelationships and some evidence to support the concepts. Newton's concept was gravity; Darwin's was natural selection.

Nor could Bowen get away with just asserting that human functioning (the word "functioning" is preferred to "behavior" because it has much broader implications) could be better understood in the context of evolutionary theory and natural systems. He too had to offer plausible concepts about how this process works and some evidence to support these concepts. One of his central concepts is the emotional system, and one of the key ways in which he provided evidence to support the concept was through the defining of functional facts in relationship systems. Bowen's evidence justified making the assumption that the human is significantly governed by the same emotional guidance system that directs other living things.

The ability to define the functional facts of relationship systems depends on the mental discipline to avoid becoming preoccupied with why something is happening, and thereby to keep the focus on what is happening. Bowen saw a process in the human family that transcends the motives of the individuals involved. The family, in other words, could be accurately conceptualized as an emotional unit. There is a predictability in the processes of human functioning and behavior equivalent to the predictability with which sunflowers follow the rays of the sun and salmon migrate up river to spawn. Focus on the what, when, where, and how of the relationship process is what permits the predictable actions and reactions in the human family to be defined sufficiently to merit considering them as facts of human functioning.

Many people think of Murray Bowen as a therapist who came up with the notion of "sending people back to their families to differentiate a self." They think of him as a pioneer in family therapy. He is. He is one of many great pioneers in the field. But all the methods and techniques of family therapy that Bowen developed are based on certain fundamental assumptions about the nature of man, assumptions that are anchored in facts of functioning that can be seen in the human family and in the larger social system. The therapy is based on the fact that not only has evolution endowed them with an automatic guidance system, it has also endowed them with the capacity to watch themselves and others—to reflect, and to abstract. In addition, it has endowed humans with the potential to define and select more options for their behavior than any other species on Earth.

It is important that we have come to honor Bowen today. I guess it means that not only do we think he has already contributed something to our individual and collective lives but, more importantly, that he is "on to something." If that is true, it will be nature that ultimately honors Bowen; just as it has honored Darwin and a number of other people who looked at something that everybody else had looked at and saw something that no one else had ever seen.

Subjectivity, Homo Sapiens and Science

Murray Bowen, MD

Early in my psychiatric career, I wondered why psychiatry was not a real science, instead of a pseudo-science governed by a "scientific method." I had no presumption about ever making a contribution in such a complex field. I was merely seeking a clarification for myself. Now, after almost forty years I am pleased with my life. To my own satisfaction, I think I know one way toward a major new theory about adjustment. The outcome may be a century away. The current situation is more chaotic than before. This might have been better predicted. I believe human behavior will eventually become a science. The major barrier appears to be subjectivity. It is part of human experience. It cannot be measured or verified. When subjectivity creeps into theoretical postulations, the result is more chaotic and less scientific. I will attempt to present a few ideas about the field.

In the twentieth century, psychiatric thinking has been based primarily on psychoanalytic theory. It considers the human as unique and different from other forms of life. The contributions from psychoanalysis have been tremendous, but it has never moved toward becoming an accepted science. I believe that has been blocked by basic formulations from literature, philosophy, mythology, and the arts. None of these disciplines came from scientific facts. All came from human experience which came originally from the brain of human beings. Anything generated in the human brain is vulnerable to feeling contamination, unless some discipline can insure reasonable objectivity. Freud was aware of the deficiencies in his theory but his followers were

Published in Volume 4, No. 2, Fall 1982.

not. They tended to treat his writings as eternal truths. Most people are not aware of the great difference between truth and fact. Truth is subjective. Fact is scientific. Practitioners are rarely aware of the small points and discipline that goes into theory or science. Psychiatric practice and research produced volumes of subjectivity. It could not pass muster in serious research. Psychologists came into the field to help with research. They developed an extremely complex scientific method designed to handle the subjectivity in a structured scientific way. They hoped it might raise the entire field to the status of a science. Debates about this have continued for decades. I do not believe human behavior can become a science as long as we use the scientific method.

In the 1940s teachers and experts could not answer specific questions about theory. I sought answers from the literature. I was on the library committee with easy access to past and present writings. My quest led through science, psychiatry, psychoanalysis, psychology, sociology, anthropology, ethology, evolution, astronomy, philosophy, mythology, physics, mathematics, biology, religion, and all the disciplines about human behavior. The basic goal was to find common denominators on which the disciplines were based.

My reading eventually led to the notion of the human as a phylogenetic development from the lower forms of life. I believed it would bring us closer to science if we could see the human as related to all other living things. It is a scientific fact the Earth is part of the larger universe; that the Earth is made up of all kinds of inorganic elements that behave according to scientific principle; and the Earth abounds in all kinds of life that came from the primordial ooze. Life is generally divided into plant life and animal life, both tied to the Earth and both intimately interlinked. All life reproduces in clearly defined cycles, changing a little with each cycle. The animal world is mobile and it includes forms that extend from bacteria and other one cell forms, to the complexity of *Homo sapiens* at the other extreme. The animal world has some kind of a nervous system that operates either by some undefined chemical mechanism or through a conglomerate of nervous tissue and chemical reaction. In its phylogenetic development, the nervous system proceeds through a series of orderly steps from the lower animals to the marvelous brain of *Homo sapiens*, about which we know too little.

In addition to *structure*, the brain includes numerous *functions* that go back to instincts and are not clearly associated with any structure. Fairly late in phylogeny, the human developed the ability to stand upright and to think, reflect, and reason. This is not meant to be specific for anatomy and physiology. It is mentioned only for comparative reasons. Slowly the human developed a spoken language, cultures, philosophies, religions, mathematics, literature, the arts, and a host of other functions more subjective than factual. Science had to have a beginning. Along the way, man learned to figure out the nature of the universe, the properties of the Earth on which he lived, and other subjects that had to do with pure science. Science worked well as long as he focused on the universe and the inanimate world. It worked less well when he focused on animal forms. It was least effective when he focused on himself. Terms developed for the pure sciences are blurred when applied to other fields. The literature and dictionaries are not clear about things such as science and theory. On a strict level, I have not considered a theory to be valid unless it can somehow be synonymous with the universe, the earth, the tides, the seasons, the predictable cycles of life, and man as a reproductive, evolving form of life. Simple analogies between one way of thinking and another way of thinking are common place. An analogy is *not* a connection.

My reading effort in the conceptual field was a part-time issue. I found no clues that could be operational in research as

long as the focus was on individual psychological theory. The
background thinking was mostly latent for years. In the mean-
while my professional work was moved to the National Institute
of Mental Health. The focus on the family instead of the individual provided a completely different thinking dimension. The
previous years of study may have figured into entire families living on the ward together. The study played a monumental part in
the research itself and in the subsequent twenty-five years. With
the families living together, I could *see* a completely different
world. Years of work suddenly became clear. The view faded in
and out until I learned to control it better. It was there when I
could think about evolution and science. It could fade when other
thoughts or emotion intervened. The view was so wondrous, I
managed to keep it most of my working hours. The new view
produced so many researchable clues, it was impossible to know
which was most important, or which could be approached in the
available time. Very early in the research, *I knew within me, the
family phenomenon would eventually lead to a different theory
about psychiatry and human adaptation.* A new theory might
not be possible for a century, but the essential variables were all
there. Research associates could not *see* what was so clear to
me. They could *see* only what previous thinking permitted them
to see. I wondered why I could see better than the others. In
retrospect it was the years of previous thinking, plus the presence of the entire families. To help the others *see*, I devised
exercises to help them to a different way of thinking. Over time,
they could *see* too. The ability to see was based on their level of
maturity and not their relationship to me. The research led automatically to a method of family therapy before it was generally
known. The family therapy was a superficial manifestation and
not a primary thing. A few other psychiatrists were also involved
in family research, mostly from a conventional perspective. They
reported their findings through individual theory. I was stuck in

regard to communicating outside the ward. I used a language on the ward that others did not understand. In professional papers, I tried to "split the difference." Don Jackson was the only other family researcher who considered theory to be important. He was thinking communications theory which was quite different.

Theory was very important to me. I had spent years working toward a scientific view of man. Every conceivable safeguard was used to keep observations on verifiable fact rather than subjective impression. My gallery of critics at NIMH helped me stay alert. Basic postulations had been based on natural systems in lower forms of life rather than general systems theory. Systems theory was used to convert certain items of subjectivity into the functional facts of systems. I have written about that. There are numerous examples, such as, "That man talks is a verifiable fact, but what he says is not a fact." Observers were not permitted to use interpretations or "loaded" words such as "depressed" in observations. Observations were based on fact, as far as discipline could go. Predictable actions that repeated over and over, in all the families, eventually found their way into concepts. Everything was based on *facts* as far as possible. Critics were fast to point out subjectivity in observer situations. Critics suggested movies as more objective. Even the best plans of researchers can go awry. A dozen observers can watch a movie and emerge with a spectrum of different observations based more on the information in the brain of the observer than the actual situation. A trained and disciplined observer can be more accurate than the average less disciplined observer. To my critics I admitted the fallacies and merely said, "We are aware of the problem and are doing our best to deal with it." The whole research stands on that effort. I believe we did a good job.

After it was possible to see the potential for theory in the research, a major goal was to package the observations as accurately as possible and preserve the clues for future research. My concepts were framed in the orientation of the human as a bio-logical-evolutionary creature. I believe the effort was fairly successful. People wondered where I had found the "intuitive" concepts. They were built into the research before it started. Work on the concepts and theory continued through subsequent years.

A detour began in 1957 which obscured the effort toward theory. John Spiegel initiated a national meeting for family researchers at the Orthopsychiatric Meeting. Family psychotherapy was mentioned in passing. The ideas of family therapy became public. The notion of family *therapy*, seen as a thing unto itself, spread like wildfire. Dozens and then hundreds began methods of family therapy based on conventional theory. At the time I believed this was healthy, and others would begin to help with theory when they could see the family phenomenon. It never occurred. The rush gained momentum. After a few years it subsided somewhat but this did not last. New people kept coming in and the rush grew to stampede proportions. People were not interested in theory. Group therapy provided a model for many. Family and group therapy were erroneously connected. Mental health people had been in it long enough to become experts. The movement surged. Counselors and people who had never previously done therapy became family therapists. Methodology became so simplistic that many assumed all they had to do was get the family together and start them communicating and emoting. Experts began touring the circuits attracting new followers. Social work and psychology students were attracted to touring lectures in droves. They were forced into eclecticism by listening to the various experts from which they fashioned their own brand of gospel. The new therapists made inroads into the time honored academic approaches of psychoanalytic institutes and departments of psychiatry. The number of family institutes ballooned. Family institutes could be started by a few experts, a meeting place, new stationery, and a few students. The situation was similar to medicine in the late nineteenth century when a few doctors with a hospital could start new medical schools which produced poorly trained doctors in volume. In the 1915 period the Flexner Committee closed the poor schools and required others to meet standards. The family therapy movement has had no controls beyond a few self-imposed controls and those are questionable. The rush to family therapy continues, as a thing unto itself, responding more to the popularity and private practice income than to the level of professionalism in the therapist.

The family therapy rush is seen more as a phenomenon in society than the action of one person or group of people. The family idea is one of the most significant contributions in this century. The need was there, social regression had increased, societal anxiety was higher, and new people rushed in to fill the gap. I think the whole thing could have been better predicted. The whole thing has the marks of a regression which will run its course and eventually settle down to a period of societal progression with a more normal course. As it stands now, people are not prepared to listen to theory, but some calmer day in the future more and more people will be attracted by the notion of human behavior eventually becoming a real science.

I believe that human behavior will one day become an accepted science that can grow and develop with all the sciences. I have presented some ideas that I hope will be helpful. When it does become a science, family concepts and relatedness to the lower forms of life will play some kind of part.

SOME ASPECTS OF SYSTEMS THINKING

MICHAEL E. KERR, MD

The ideas presented were stimulated, in part, by a recent reading of the book, *A Feeling for the Organism*, by Evelyn Fox Keller. The book is a biography of Barbara McClintock that places particular emphasis on her professional life. Several years ago Dr. McClintock was awarded the Nobel Prize for her pioneering work on genetics.

A part of the book I found especially interesting was a description of the difficulty most of McClintock's scientific colleagues had accepting her radically new ideas. This resulted in her most important research findings being discounted for over twenty years. Were other scientists unable to accept McClintock's ideas because she could not communicate them clearly or was it because they were unable to listen? Indeed, her work is complex, requiring considerable intellectual discipline to follow the painstaking steps of her research, but its complexity was probably not the main obstacle to its being understood and accepted. Almost certainly, the main obstacle was the tacit assumptions of her colleagues about the nature of genes. The facts about genetics revealed by McClintock's study of maize contradicted widely held beliefs about how genes functioned. Historically, when newly discovered facts have contradicted accepted beliefs about the natural world, the beliefs have yielded their grasp on human thinking very slowly. The resistance that McClintock encountered is similar to that experienced by other scientific pioneers.

Published in Volume 9, No. 4, Fall 1988.

This paper is based on a presentation made at the Clinical Conference Series on May 21, 1988.

After reading about McClintock's difficulty being "heard," I began to wonder about how effective I have been at communicating my understanding of families. When I listen to family members and watch them interact, I see an orderly, predictable, and fairly uncomplicated process. I think elements that are basic to the patterns of emotional functioning in human families are easily observed in subhuman species. Do others see what I see? Have I been able to describe clearly what I see? Rather than discuss specific concepts in systems theory, I will concentrate on some important, overall aspects of systems thinking. I hope my presentation will stimulate you to make some of your assumptions about the nature of human emotional functioning and behavior more explicit. Failure to define one's assumptions adequately is an important obstacle to changing from an individual, cause and effect model to a systems model in reference to human behavior.

It is difficult to think "systems" consistently. An ever present "emotional undertow" undermines people's ability to see a self-reinforcing relationship process that transcends blame. On the contrary, emotionality inclines people to ascribe cause to one or a few elements in that process. People can learn to think systems more consistently, but it requires more than an intellectual effort. An emotional change is needed. Whether an emotional change occurs depends on a person's willingness to engage the important people and issues that he would rather avoid. The alternative to engagement is cutoff. Emotional cutoff can provide comfort, but it forecloses the chance to learn about emotional systems and the factors that govern one's vulnerability to them. In addition, emotional cutoff often provides comfort in the short run, but not in the long run.

I will begin the discussion of aspects of systems thinking by defining some terms. Several years ago, Bowen defined *science, theory,* and *subjectivity.* As a consequence, these became watch-words at the Family Center. However, these terms have frequently been used by many of us without precise definition. I think it is important for me to define these terms more carefully, particu-larly since I have helped make them watchwords at Georgetown. I hope my effort to be more precise will stimulate your thinking about these areas.

I will begin with science. The definition of science I will present is taken from a book, *The Scale of Nature,* by Dr. John Tyler Bonner, Professor of Biology at Princeton University, and Distinguished Guest Lecturer for this year's Family Symposium. The definition is as follows:

> Science is about things. It is about rocks, stars, atoms, and living beings. It is about all those things which surround us and which used to be called Nature with a capital N. Further-more, it is about the relation of things. Science is concerned with order.[1]

Bonner's description of science is similar to one presented by Bowen at the 1982 Family Symposium. Bowen distinguished between that which is a *production of the human brain* and that which *exists independent of the brain.* The latter is the realm of science, a realm that is not constrained or defined by what we think or say about it. Man and his brain are part of science, but the brain's productions are not. If man becomes extinct, the realm of science will be changed little by that extinction. Defining science is important because family systems theory assumes that it will be possible to develop a science of human behavior, along with astronomy, biology, chemistry, geology, and physics.

---

[1] John Tyler Bonner. 1969. *The Scale of Nature.* New York: Harper and Row, p. 22.

Science is distinct from the *scientific method*. Professor Bonner makes this distinction as follows:

> The pursuit of science is a human undertaking entirely delineated by the mind of man [2]. . . . The formal approach to science is founded upon a scientific method which is a set of rules that comply with common sense. This has become the province of philosophy, and the philosophers have devised a grammar of scientific usage which, in its pure form, is a scientific method. This is sometimes called the philosophy of science, and various approaches have specific names, such as logic, logical positivism, symbolic logic, and others. But . . . these approaches are no more science than the English language or mathematics.[3]

The scientific method is used to gain knowledge about science. Its application, however, is not the only path to knowledge about science. Other paths exist for knowing about the factual world. Nor does the application of the scientific method guarantee contact with the realm of science. Bowen has made this point by saying, "One cannot chi-square a feeling and get a fact." Rigorous statistical evaluation of subjective data, in other words, does not produce an objective conclusion.

When sufficient facts have been defined about a segment of the natural world, it is then possible to construct a *scientific theory*. Theory is a generalization that attempts to define an order to what has been described factually. Relationships are theorized to exist between events. Theory is not science, and if it is not equated with science, it is open to change. New facts can modify it. If theory is equated with science, however, it becomes dogma. Supporters of dogma ignore facts that contradict it which precludes any possibility for change.

---

[2] Bonner, p. 18.
[3] Bonner, p. 21.

A *scientist* attempts not to ignore any fact about the natural world that is inconsistent with accepted theory. He modifies his theory rather than dismiss a newly discovered, errant fact. Barbara McClintock is a "true" scientist whose mental discipline permitted her to see beyond conventional theory's conception of the genome. Scientists are not confined to research laboratories. In a sense, anyone who is aware of the distinctions between fact, dogma, and theory and who is guided accordingly might be considered a scientist. By this definition, family therapists can be scientists. Although mental health professionals are steeped in truth and dogma, which makes it difficult for them to distinguish between knowledge and belief, they can learn to make these distinctions more consistently.

Family systems theory was designed to be consistent with known facts about natural systems. Bowen has not claimed complete success, but the development of a theory that is consistent with the facts has been his goal. He has written extensively about what is involved in attempting to move towards science. Like all theories, family systems theory is not science but a creation of the human brain. It conceptualizes a relationship between the known facts about human emotional functioning and behavior. The degree to which the theoretical concepts are linked to these facts is the degree to which it is a scientific theory.

The terms *subjectivity* and *objectivity* are also important to define. Some argue that all knowledge about the natural world is subjective because all sensory stimuli are processed through the nervous system. As a consequence, the world is neither seen nor heard as it is, but only as the nervous system records it to be. This is a broad definition of subjectivity. Subjectivity can be more narrowly defined as that which arises from "conditions" within the brain and sense organs and not directly caused by external stimuli. The important point to recognize is that the "conditions" within the brain and sense organs can vary in the following ways: (1) differences exist among individuals in the "conditions" that are average for their brains over time, and (2) "conditions" in the same brain may fluctuate widely. The "conditions" of the brain and sense organs are influenced by factors such as emotional and feeling states and beliefs about the way things are.

Objectivity can also be defined broadly or more restrictively. A broad definition is that which exists independent of the perceptions provided by the mind and senses. This is equivalent to a definition of science. A more restrictive definition of objectivity is that which belongs to the sensible world, that which we perceive through our senses. When objectivity and subjectivity are defined more narrowly, it eliminates a dichotomy between them. Rather than a dichotomy, objective and subjective perceptions constitute a continuum. At the objective end of the continuum, perceptions of the natural world are observable and verifiable. This is the domain of facts and knowledge. At the subjective end of the continuum, perceptions are neither observable nor verifiable. This is the domain of imagination, truth, and belief. The relative influence of objectivity and subjectivity on perception varies at gradations between these extremes. An individual's position on the continuum is determined by the "conditions" of his brain and sense organs.

Science is not equivalent to objectivity, but knowledge about science is assembled through objectivity. Subjectivity may have a role in the making of scientific discoveries, but there is a distinction between the process of discovery and the discovery itself. A belief is a lens through which we look at the world. If that belief is not equated with the world itself, it can make us alert to events that contradict the validity of the belief. To move toward the realm of science, however, beliefs must be replaced by factual knowledge.

As far as we know, *Homo sapiens* is the only species that can distinguish between objectivity and subjectivity. This ability is a function of the intellectual system. Bowen termed the ability to be relatively objective about emotionality, *emotional objectivity*. Human beings can be actively involved in an emotional system and, at the same time, recognize the nature of that involvement, both in its effects on themselves and on others. Distinguishing between objectivity and subjectivity is a prerequisite for modifying one's basic level of differentiation of self. This is because subjectivity is so strongly influenced by the relationship system. People cannot change in relationship to others (become better defined selves) without becoming clearer about the subjective nature of their assumptions about themselves and others.

The difference between cause and effect thinking and systems thinking is another important area. Systems thinking is concerned with *how, what, when,* and *where* events occur. It is not concerned with *why* they occur. Focus on why an event occurs automatically converts thinking from a systems to a cause and effect mode. A simple example will illustrate this. A husband says to his wife, "I react to what I perceive as your disapproving look." This statement can be consistent with systems thinking. In contrast, if the husband says, "I react because of your disapproving look," it reflects cause and effect thinking. The distinction is fairly obvious. The first statement describes what happens without assigning blame to either spouse. The second statement asserts why something happens ("because of") and, in this case, blames the wife. Statements about how, what, when, and where describe a process, a sequence of events. Statements about why assign cause to one element in that sequence. A systems model neither defines the wife's disapproving look to be the cause of her husband's reaction (for example, becoming unduly quiet) nor does it define the husband's reaction to be the cause of the wife's disapproving look. A systems model defines a self-reinforcing process based on mutual participation.

People can learn to be less emotionally reactive without giving up cause and effect thinking. They do this when they learn emotional "detachment" as a technique, as a way of coping with emotionally charged situations. If emotional detachment is learned as a technique, however, it will quickly evaporate when anything unexpected is encountered. In contrast to training one-self to be less reactive, one can become less reactive automatically based on a shift from cause and effect to systems thinking about one's relationships. A shift in a way of thinking occurs only gradually, but the emotional detachment it provides can withstand intense and unpredictable emotional situations. Systems thinking defines a process, a process extending beyond one individual to a relationship, beyond one relationship to a triangle, beyond one triangle to interlocking triangles in the nuclear family, beyond nuclear family relationships to relationships in the multigenerational family, beyond the family to the social system, and beyond the human to the subhuman world. Successful efforts toward more differentiation of self depend on emotional detachment being based on a way of thinking, not a technique.

The final aspect of systems thinking that I will discuss is *functioning position*. Man builds mechanical systems to perform certain functions. If a person who is ignorant about engines is given a carburetor, he can only describe the carburetor's structure. He can have no notion about its function. However, if given an engine without a carburetor, he can study the operation of the engine and determine the missing functions. Once these functions are defined, he could design a piece of equipment to perform them. His design may not resemble a conventional carburetor, but that is of no consequence.

The interrelationship of structure and function is more complicated in living systems. Changes in function can alter structure and changes in structure can alter function in mechanical systems, but the alterations are irreversible. Living systems, in contrast, have remarkable flexibility. Not only can structure alter function and function alter structure, but the changes are often reversible. Alteration of structure based on alteration of function, and the reversal of structural change in response to functional change, is what I interpret Murray Bowen to mean by "functional dysfunction." A muscle atrophies if it is not used, but much or all of the atrophy is reversible if the muscle is exercised. Chronic psychosis and associated changes in biochemical structures can be precipitated by poor functioning and reversed by improved functioning. The behavior of cancer cells can be linked to changes in cell structure, but these changes in structure can also be precipitated by changes in cell function. There is considerable evidence that structure and function are in a state of dynamic equilibrium in living systems. Most symptoms that are attributed to irreversible disturbances in structure may actually reflect potentially reversible disturbances in function.

In reference to human diseases, it is often difficult to conceive of a disturbance in structure as reflecting a disturbance in function. Professional training, popular literature, and conventional wisdom condition us to believe that parts of the human body malfunction because they are defective. Aberrant behavior is ascribed to abnormal personality structure or head trauma, disturbed kidney function is attributed to kidney disease, and psychosis is frequently attributed to brain pathology. A systems model does not discount the role that disturbances in structure can have in symptom development, but the disturbances are viewed in larger context. The relationship system governs the functioning of individuals (to a variable degree depending on basic level of differentiation), the functioning of individuals governs the functioning of their physical and psychological systems, the functioning of physical and psychological systems governs the structure of those systems, and vice versa. Parts of the body can become defective, but the impact of the defect on the functioning of the individual and his relationship system is influenced by variables that extend far beyond the defect itself.

The fact that function can regulate structure and that functioning position can regulate function explains the characteristics of triangles. Each "point" of a triangle is a position of functioning. In a triangle, a person is not an individual but an extension of the emotional system. If one member of a triangle alters his functioning, the functioning of the other members changes automatically. Functioning positions in triangles can become relatively fixed. Their fixed nature accentuates the personality characteristics of the people occupying the various positions. Commonly, the nature of the triangle is attributed to the personality characteristics of its members. In actuality, personality characteristics are strongly influenced by the nature of the triangle. (Function can regulate structure.) A common clinical example illustrates this point. A person described his father as cold and distant, his mother as warm and close. He viewed himself as suffering the consequences of exposure to an overinvolved mother and an underinvolved father. This person views the personality characteristics of his parents as governing the nature of the triangle. His thinking is cause and effect. A systems model explains the characteristics of each parent on the basis of how they function in relationship to each other. The "warmer" the mother is, the "colder" the father is, and vice versa. The son's anger at his father and sympathy toward his mother (an aspect of his functioning position) accentuates the polarization in parental personalities, further solidifying the triangle.

A shift from cause and effect thinking to systems thinking in reference to human behavior creates new options for change. One's own personality and functioning need not be constrained by the nature of the triangles in which one is embedded. An awareness of the reciprocity in human emotional functioning, an ability to see oneself as part of the system, and the motivation to change oneself and not others, frees people to be themselves.

REFERENCES

Keller, Evelyn Fox. 1983. *A Feeling for the Organism*. New York: W. H. Freeman and Company.

Universal Autism: Extinction Resulting from Failure to Develop Relationships

John B. Calhoun, PhD

REVIEWED BY

Daniel V. Papero, PhD, MSSW

As early as 1956, Calhoun was interested in and thinking about research where he could pin down the relationship of residential stability to behavioral disturbance and social cohesion. By the 1960s, such research became possible.

Dr. Calhoun's preliminary research (1968-1973) allowed populations of mice and rats to reproduce in a closed environment, a habitat or "universe" from which no escape was possible. The animals were free from climatic hardship and predation and were supplied with adequate nesting space and food. All the research populations eventually came to a point where the young did not reach reproductive maturity and the population became extinct.

The last generation of subjects was born as the adult population neared a density eight times the optimum. Preceding generations had displayed intense competition for the small number of social roles available as the crowded conditions intensified. These animals generally failed to attain a social position and became withdrawn and inactive. Members of the final generation, however, neither fought, nor competed, nor mated. Dubbed the

Published in Volume 7, No. 2, Spring 1986.

On April 2, 1986 John B. Calhoun, PhD, Director of the Unit for Research on Behavioral Systems, Laboratory of Clinical Sciences, Intramural Research Program, National Institute of Mental Health, presented his paper at the Family Center's Distinguished Scientist Lecture Series.

beautiful ones for their unscarred pelage, these animals appeared to remain at an immature stage of development beyond which they could not proceed.

The males of this generation spent much of their time lined up on partitions within the habitat. They sat with their sides touching and had little interest in the world around them. Calhoun believed their behavioral development had become arrested at about sixteen days of age, an infantile stage marked by close body contact within the litter. Calhoun referred to these males as *barflies*. Females appeared to develop somewhat further. Their behavior became fixed in an early juvenile stage, about forty-five days of age. This stage is marked by environmental exploration and curiosity about strange objects. Calhoun called these animals *pied pipers*, because of their tendency to orient themselves to and to follow the experimenter (a strange object) as he moved about the universe. The inability of this generation to form and maintain relationships led Calhoun to designate the beautiful ones *autistic*. That all members of the generation were thus incapacitated justified the adjective *universal*. The state of universal autism culminates in the extinction of the population.

Calhoun reported that he had been unprepared conceptually for the appearance of the autistic generation. In the following years he attempted to determine how to continue the direction of his research. By 1975, he began a new phase of research to determine if there was any way to increase the population to eight times optimal density *without* all individuals becoming autistic.

Certain changes were made in the design of the habitat itself. Two different strains of mice were bred to create genetic diversity and greater adaptability. The light source was modified to present twelve two-hour episodes of graduated changes in light intensity. This approximated the waxing and waning of natural daylight, allowing the animals to be oriented in time as well as in space. In addition, the time between generations was increased from 100 to 200 days. This gave females more time to develop effective maternal behavior.

Finally, the food supply was altered to make the level of vitamin A comparable to that found naturally in the environment. This modification resulted from a fortuitous discovery that commercial feed had a vitamin A level twelve times the natural level. In subsequently studying the effects of heightened vitamin A consumption on subject populations, Calhoun learned that increased levels of the vitamin led to what he termed *perceptual blindness*. In essence, the animals ceased to notice and respond appropriately to the characteristics of their associates. In previous studies, Calhoun had determined that vitamin A storage doubles when the population reaches about five times optimal density. This may represent a temporary mechanism for survival in the heightened density, but animals of this generation did not conceive and remained permanently damaged. In short, Calhoun realized that increased vitamin A consumption due to dietary enhancement actually produced the same sort of impairment as crowding. Increasing levels of vitamin A was equivalent to increasing population density.

With the modifications noted above, populations were again allowed to expand. At two times optimal density, the first signs of trouble developed. At this stage, autistic males or barflies began to appear. The changes seemed to assist the females in maintaining themselves longer. By generation six, however, females began to have great difficulty rearing young. They ultimately were able to rear offspring, but not in sufficient numbers to double the population again. By generation seven, females did not take care of their young, who typically disappeared around three days of age. Even when, at this point, population was reduced to a level at which animals had been reasonably successful at reproducing before, there was no recovery. Even though adequate space was available, the remaining animals crowded themselves by moving into the same nest spaces. When animals were removed from the environment and were placed in a new habitat, some recovered reproductive ability. As long as they were in the original closed universe, however, no recovery occurred.

In February 1986, Calhoun was able to generate a graph from the research data which showed the correlation between residential stability and behavioral disturbance and social cohesion. Residential stability remained high (ninety-seven percent for females and slightly lower for males) until the point of twice optimal density. At this point (generation three), residential stability began to decline sharply and autism began among the males. The females quickly followed suit. Each generation declined further. By generation seven (four generations after twice optimal density) the animals were completely unaware of anything in their environment. The autism was universal.

Due to the time frame of the lecture, Dr. Calhoun passed quickly over the remaining points in his paper. The first addressed his concept of social velocity in relation to the development and meaning of universal autism. Within an optimally sized group of about twelve adults, individuals differ from one another in the total number of times each member is active and alert. The more active and alert an individual, the more likely the individual is to form relationships with others. Because of the correlation between activity and the opportunity for social relationships, Calhoun refers to the measurement as *social velocity*.

Within the optimal size group, the social velocity of each member can be plotted, resulting in a straight line with a relatively smooth distribution of individuals along the line from the highest ranking individual to the lowest. Differences in velocity between individuals reflect comparable differences in behavior. These behavioral differences are marked enough that even adjacently ranked individuals can recognize one another. Each individual is able to perform a distinct role within the group. As group size exceeds the optimum, however, animals in increasing numbers lose their separate behavioral identities. Fewer and fewer are able to retain normal velocities and more become part of an indistinguishable mass at the lowest end of the curve. As population increases, therefore, optimal group size decreases. Fewer and fewer functional roles are available. Calhoun suggests that rising population density increases the intensity of social interaction while reducing the optimal group size. He concludes:

> . . . a threefold increase in group size above the optimum can produce biochemical and behavioral changes comparable to those accompanying subspecific differentiation through natural selection and gene drift.

Turning at this point to human development, Calhoun commented on the Von Foerster equation which closely matches the estimated numbers of humans over the past 2000 years. The Von Foerster curve indicates that each successive doubling of the human population requires half the time of the preceding doubling. Such an accelerating increase, if sustained, would jump to infinity in 2026 A.D. Such increasing density is thought to have been possible through the creation of new ideas and consequent social roles which allow more people to survive and function. Currently the world population is approaching 1,000 times that of 43,000 BP. Calhoun refers to increased information, creativity, and roles as *conceptual space*. In essence, therefore, conceptual space and population have increased together.

Calhoun's calculations suggest to him that the expansion of conceptual space is slowing and approaching the status of a constant. Population is in the meantime increasing, although at a slower rate than that predicted by the Von Foerster curve. That equation broke in the years 1975-76. This corresponds to the animal model at the point when the population passes twice optimal density. Calhoun also notes that this same time (at least for the population of the United States) represents the approximate time by which most maturing individuals will have been exposed their entire lifetime to a level of vitamin A comparable to that producing autism in the animal populations studied.

In the animal studies, the point of no return from universal autism occurred somewhere between two and a half and four generations past twice optimal density. This of course presupposes no escape from the habitat or milieu, which is the current status of the human on the planet. Assuming a human generation to be twenty-seven years in length, the point of no return from universal autism for the human falls between 2042 and 2083. The mean date, 2063, corresponds exactly to independent calculations of peak world population. Consequently, the next 200 to 400 years represents a transitional period for the human species when the processes which have permitted population growth become rapidly ineffective and before a new phase and mechanism can come into play. Calhoun believes this period of transition will be difficult, although there may be some things which will assist the species through the difficulty.

While pursuing his research with expanding populations and universal autism, Calhoun has also been pursuing two other projects. In the first he has attempted to investigate the "role of acquisition of collaborative behavior by rats in (a) inhibiting of origin of pathologies arising from increase in density above the optimum while simultaneously (b) modifying the function of the brain to enable the rats to develop more complex and longer conceptualization and behaviors." In the second project he has focused on the development of prosthetic strategies which would simulate brain functions and foster the further development of "evolutionary intelligence." Such devices would allow the human to bring together rapidly and effectively the sum of all previously expressed thought providing new ways of evaluating consensus and finding creative solutions to problems.

The results of this research were not presented formally during the April 2 lecture but represent lines of thought and experimentation which may provide directions and mechanisms to help man avoid universal autism—if the animal model can be applied to humans. The effort with teaching collaborative behavior to rats led to the insight that prior acquisition of collaborative social roles alters central nervous system functioning. Such alteration permits behavioral states to continue longer than otherwise. Longer lasting behavioral states permit more complex and more diverse interaction with associates. Such complicated experimental interaction reflects richer and more complex thought processes. If this theoretical viewpoint is correct, it will support the importance of the abundance and breadth of social roles in preventing universal autism. Calhoun believes himself to be in a position to begin the work necessary to determine if this theory is correct.

A question and answer period followed the formal presentation. During this period Dr. Calhoun was able to expand upon several points. In his view, the current ecological interdependency of all people on the planet has resulted in identifying compassion and self-interest. Because all are affected by what happens to another, compassion and self-interest become identical.

A question about the manifestations of perceptual blindness in humans led Dr. Calhoun to suggest that the individual may become blind to the ideas surrounding him. It becomes difficult or impossible to see the relationship between ideas. He stated that the dilemma may already be present in science. He commented on the difference between "rich" and "minimal" theories. A rich theory encompasses many parameters and a broad range of ideas and, therefore, is difficult to investigate. A minimal theory focuses on the smallest unit which can be definitively managed, providing limited answers in a brief time. Minimal theories may lead to minimal standards, which quickly are adopted as standard.

After the formal discussion, the audience was invited to pursue questions informally with Dr. Calhoun at a reception in his honor. Many accepted and discussion continued on into the evening.

THE PRESS OF POPULATION

KATHLEEN B. KERR, MSN, MA

It is axiomatic that we are in no way protected from the consequences of our actions by remaining confused about the ecological meaning of our humanness, ignorant of ecological processes, and unmindful of the ecological aspects of history. I
have tried to show the real nature of humanity's predicament
not because understanding its nature will enable us to escape
it, but because if we do not understand it we shall continue to
act and react in ways that make it worse.[1]

Thus begins the preface of *Overshoot* by William Catton,
teacher and writer of human ecology and environmental sociology. This book puts in ecological terms the two million years of
human cultural evolution. In particular it focuses on the repeti-
tive processes of humans "taking over additional portions of the
Earth's total life supporting capacity, at the expense of other creatures."[2] Each time this has occurred, by taming fire or developing tools, horticulture, metallurgy, agriculture, technology, or
medicine, human population has increased dramatically. However, the latest way human population has expanded can lead to the

---

Published in Volume 14, No. 2, Spring 1993.

*This paper incorporated reviews of two presentations at the Thursday
Professional Lecture Series, one by Nancy Wallace on March 11, 1993
entitled "Systems Dynamics of Human Population" and the other by
Dr. Geza Teleki in February 1993 entitled "Chimpanzee Conservation."*

[1] William Catton. 1982. *Overshoot: The Ecological Basis of Revolutionary Change.* Urbana: University of Illinois Press, p. vii.

[2] Catton, p. 5.

end of the process. Catton sees the last four centuries of human progress and population increase as facilitated by the discovery of a new hemisphere and the development of ways to use the Earth's fossil fuel reservoirs. Both of these events are non-repeatable. Humans are now using the resources of future generations to support a population that has overshot the carrying capacity of the planet.

In the forward to *Overshoot*, Stewart Udall describes the latest version of this process in the United States. The United States came out of World War II infatuated with science and its unlocking of atomic energy. It believed science could solve any physical problem including future energy supplies. In the mid-twentieth century the United States was convinced that "free" cheap atomic energy would eliminate resource shortages anywhere on Earth allowing man freedom from limits. The main obstacle to this freedom was the restricted amount of science and technology manpower available.

The posture toward natural resources shifted from conservation of scarce resources to "the wise management of plenty" advocated in a 1962 report for President Kennedy of a special committee of the National Academy of Sciences. This report epitomized the belief in omnipotent science and in an age where there were no problems, only technical solutions. Exhaustion of natural resources would be handled by the discovery or synthesis of cheaper, better substitutes. Udall sees this euphoria reaching its zenith with the successful landing of astronauts on the moon in 1969.

Then in the 1970s the reappearance of famines in Africa and Asia, the oil embargo, and the natural gas shortage all questioned these assumptions of the 1950s and 1960s. These events suggest a re-evaluation of how much of our technological progress has been based on the availability of cheap energy. Udall concludes that evidence suggests "we have consistently exaggerated the contributions of technological genius and underestimated the contributions of natural resources." [3]

Nancy Wallace, the Washington Director of the International Population Program at the Sierra Club introduced the work of Catton, Udall and others during the Thursday Professional Lecture of March 11. In her lecture entitled "Systems Dynamics of Human Population" she presented an overview of world population. She maintains that population growth is one of the biggest factors in American society today, exerting more effects than can be imagined. Population change is a large wave phenomenon happening on a slow time scale in history and only seen over decades. For example, the United States' population has tripled in this century.

Wallace discussed the effects of population on the environment. Most scientists, Wallace reported, would say the human is presently over the carrying capacity of planet Earth. Carrying capacity for any species is the number that can be supported without permanent harm to the ecosystem. For example, the ecosystem can restore itself from temporary overgrazing, but destruction of the rootlets under the soil line leads to a permanent process of desertification. This conclusion is based on levels of two resources: energy and ground water. Energy usage has depleted finite sources of fossil fuel. We are not living on the solar energy coming in each year but are using irreplaceable energy of the past. Likewise we are draining ground water from existing aquifers holding supplies from thousands of years ago. The water table in central Arizona has dropped approximately 150 feet in the last thirty years. Closer to home, the Washington Suburban Sanitary Commission estimates that the metropolitan area will begin to run out of water in 2004. A drop in the water table below the roots of large trees is a first step toward desertification.

---

[3] Catton, p. xv.

When these trees die, the understory and grasses are unable to maintain themselves in the glare of the sun and die. Without the grass roots to hold organic matter, soil becomes sand. Historically, desertification has occurred as humans have pushed areas on the planet beyond their carrying capacity. Societies living in these areas at these times have crashed. Easter Island, North Africa, Mesopotamia, the Middle East, and the Mayan Empire are examples. Some sections of desert in the U.S. are results of such processes. Evidence for global desertification is that currently there are twenty-four billion tons less topsoil on the planet each year.

Wallace presented a number of other environmental effects on population pressure. Methane, carbon dioxide, and nitrous oxide gases contribute to global warming. Many by-products of increased population, especially deforestation, fuel the extinction of species. Forests are being cut because of settlement, collection of wood, and sale of lumber. Desertification occurs primarily by overgrazing and cutting of wood for fuel. Increased population leads to all these effects, especially by deforestation and desertification. These, in turn, decrease the food supply needed for increased population, thereby promoting famine and increased susceptibility to disease, both of which lead to increased mortality. Wallace described a process whereby increased population drives both effects and then programs to deal with the effects, leading in systematic fashion to more and more environmental degradation. She noted, however, that not every environmental issue is a population problem. Some are results of technology, such as chlorofluorocarbons, toxic waste, and nuclear waste.

Wallace then addressed the societal effects of increased population. She described the multiplier effect whereby one variable driven by rising population increases another one even more, which increases another variable even more. She presented an example whereby a two percent annual increase in population can lead to a 200 percent increase in air pollution in twenty years. Constant change driven by an exponential growth rate in population challenges behavior patterns laid down at lower density levels. Constant crisis becomes the norm as problems and their magnitude multiply. The rate of increase in problems outstrips programs via sheer numbers and the multiplier effect. Psychological stress increases, especially in urban areas. Lack of hope becomes endemic as resources are spent in an attempt to keep up with population growth rather than to improve the quality of life. Most indicators of quality of life are going down in countries with increasing population. (Wallace spoke of the need for better quality of life indicators and the necessity for a better way of accounting. She suggested examples such as housing rehabilitations instead of housing starts and long-term rather than short-term business performance.) There is an undermining of authority, especially in areas of urbanization. Finally there is increasing disparity in wealth. High fertility societies have increasing disparity between the wealthy and the poor. The more children per family, the more difficulty they have escaping poverty.

In her summary Wallace described us as stealing from our past and our future. We are using fossil fuel and ground water, the nonrenewable resources from the past. We are degrading topsoil which has a long regeneration time and therefore will not be available to the immediate future for generations.

In the February Thursday Professional Lecture Dr. Geza Teleki, in addressing "Chimpanzee Conservation" presented a case study of the African continent which demonstrated many of the points presented. Teleki is scientific conservationist at the Committee for Conservation and Care of Chimpanzees. He noted that the way the chimp goes is likely the way the human population will go. The chimp just exemplifies the problems all species face, including humans. Given the destruction of its native African equatorial forest, current prospects for the survival of the chimp are not promising.

Teleki's career in research, wildlife and land conservation in Africa began in 1968 just after many countries gained independence. In 1968, there were half as many humans in the equatorial belt of the continent as today. By the year 2020, there will be twice as many again. He observed that the good effects of the colonial government persisted and the bad environmental effects were quickly reversed. Since then, in his view, Africa has slid backwards.

Teleki described the issues in Africa as complicated and difficult to fix. The African people themselves are stripping their countries of their assets. Both farmers pressured by subsistent needs and purposeful greedy leaders engage in consuming natural resources. A corporate element drives a process where a few, often from outside the continent, benefit from the sales of animals, trees, minerals, and cash crops. A country's natural resources are removed with little direct benefit to the country. For example, a large mahogany tree nets the country $200-$300 but the wood sells in Europe for about $300,000. Political colonialism has been replaced by economic colonialism. Foreigners trying to "help" are not always helpful. For example, religious missionaries are often avid hunters, and religious policy toward population control can counteract a country's public policy efforts. AID programs designed to be beneficial see little of their funds actually reach the target country due to administrative costs and graft in the country.

In terms of the ecological state of the continent, Teleki reported that in earlier times there were few people and much wildlife. Now there are many people and markedly decreasing wildlife. There has been large scale burning of forests. The eastern and western portions of the belt of equatorial forest are burned off. Slash and burn agriculture generates ash that temporarily improves the thin tropical soil. However, the soil quickly becomes depleted of nutrients by agricultural use. The lophira tree that readily regrows in depleted soil is fire resistant, has no fruits or buds, and contains chemicals that discourage growth of other plants or trees. Thus it contributes little or nothing to the ecosystem. Much of West Africa is now covered by this "green desert" where wildlife is absent and even farmers have abandoned the land.

After the forest is cleared, domestic animals are often introduced, preventing regrowth of vegetation. Reserves set aside in colonial times for future use are being partitioned for exploitation. The people's belief that the lands are their tribal areas and the burgeoning population's need for food also affect land use. There is also the necessity to supplement the meager diet of most people with meat and vegetable matter from nature. Meat is so scarce in Africa that most of the animal protein now comes from fish.

Commercialization of hunting puts added pressure on wildlife beyond killing for subsistence. Ecotourism increases the number of humans in relation to the animals. For the chimpanzees it may introduce a disease process similar to what happened to Native Americans when they had contact with European explorers. Urbanization leads to increased need for food for the people living in cities who are not producing their own food. It also leads to urban blight. Increased travel leads to more roads which increase accessibility of areas to tourists, hunters, miners, and loggers. With roads also comes religion. Europeans generally came by boat to coastal areas. Moslems came through the Sahara to the center. Teleki noted that their dietary regulations and beliefs about primates, along with their neutrality toward nature, led to more nature reserves in Moslem areas. Christianity, he observed, sets man apart from nature and has produced fewer nature reserves in the areas where it dominates.

Teleki discussed even more variables affecting the African situation. He noted that the female is not involved in decisions yet does the majority of work to feed the average family.

The women live with the challenge of providing firewood and food for their families but are not usually active in policy decisions and program design to manage shortages of these items. In fact, Wallace noted African women as a relatively untapped conservation resource and mentioned an unusual reforestation program designed and run by a woman. Teleki also commented on what he called complicating variables. Mechanized agriculture, which is an "improvement," destroys more of the environment and requires high expenditures for machinery, fertilizer, and hybrid seed for its continuation. Another example is the introduction of non-indigenous varieties of chickens that lay bigger eggs but need special feed and antibiotics, and are not predator evasive. Wallace noted how introducing non-indigenous varieties of cattle has led to more destruction of the environment. These cattle are heavier than native stock and exert more pressure on their hooves, killing more plant rootlets and contributing to desertification. The lesson is that every action taken by humans often has counterproductive by-products.

Africans have been interested in education, and the conservation movement there has employed it quite extensively. However, those Africans educated beyond high school tend to emigrate. Also the general population is outbreeding the educational system. The numbers of children being produced are larger than the educational system can manage. Again, Wallace had noted that if families only had the number of children for whom they could afford the relatively low school fees, gains might be made in education and population management.

Teleki gave some more specific information on chimp conservation and concluded with several interesting thoughts. He suggested we might each contribute to the world situation by persuading a child to join an occupation that doesn't degrade the environment. When asked what might help Africa, he suggested that honorable people go there and set an example by the way they live, rather than by hitting people with a message. He noted that people in Africa seem amazingly interested in learning from others.

These were both powerful, informative presentations highlighting the press of population on the planet. It is this kind of perspective and information that Bowen took into account when he developed the concept of societal regression. He posited that the anxiety of mankind, accelerated by the absence of a frontier to expand and depletion of the planet's natural resources, is feeding a societal regression (1978). The regression manifests itself in an increase in reactive behavior akin to what occurs in a family under conditions of increased anxiety. The theoretical link between behavior in a family and behavior in society is that both are emotional systems. Families and societies behave in predictable, instinctively-driven ways under varying conditions. The predictability of the behavior is based on an understanding of what happens when organisms unite in groups. The interdependency of the group allows the emergence of processes that are a property of the system rather than of the individuals who compose it. The processes are a product of the emotional system.

Bowen was familiar with the work of Calhoun (1962) and drew upon it in formulating his concepts about society. Calhoun studied the behavior of mice and rats in enclosed "universes" that foreclosed migration. He allowed density to build and observed the social, emotional, and physiological sequellae. The social pathologies that developed included increased hyperactivity, aggression, violence, cannibalism, homosexuality, pansexuality, apathy, and decreased care of the young. The populations concluded in a state of "universal autism," where they ceased reproducing and crashed. Catton (p. 107) references Calhoun's work and urges that unless we conceptualize ourselves as a species which behaves in basically the same ways as Calhoun's mice and rats we will not understand what we are experiencing.

A steady stream of studies supports the evaluation that we are in a societal regression. A recent report by Bennett evaluating American society on a number of indicators concluded that we are in a decline (1993). Whitehead, in the lead article in *The Atlantic Monthly,* details the evidence that family dissolution by divorce or illegitimacy is having profound effects on the next generation (April 1993). However, what is missing from these reports is an understanding of what powers the breakdown of society. If Calhoun, Catton, and Bowen are accurate, humans are currently behaving the way any anxious crowded species behaves. If Wallace and Teleki are accurate, a major question is, Will the human experience a population crash or purposefully reduce his density before he destroys the planet?

REFERENCES

Bennett, William J. March 1993. *The Index of Leading Cultural Indicators.* Washington, DC: Empower America, The Heritage Foundation, and The Free Congress Foundation.

Bowen, Murray. 1978. *Family Therapy in Clinical Practice.* New York: Jason Aronson, Inc.

Catton, William. 1982. *Overshoot: The Ecological Basis of Revolutionary Change.* Urbana: University of Illinois Press.

Calhoun, John B. February, 1962. "Population Density and Social Pathology." *Scientific American* 206:139-48.

Whitehead, B. D. April, 1993. "Dan Quayle Was Right." *The Atlantic Monthly* 271:47-84.

Natural Selection Theory and the Emotional System

Michael E. Kerr, MD

Family systems theory describes precise, predictable patterns of human emotional functioning and behavior. These patterns are assumed to be embedded in an emotional system that is a product of man's evolutionary heritage. An important question raised by Bowen's description of these patterns is whether their existence is consistent with present evolutionary theory. Is the evolutionary outcome of the human family being an emotional unit, a unit governed by the counterbalancing life forces of *individuality* and *togetherness*, consistent with what is known about how natural selection shapes evolutionary change?

Research by biologist Leo Buss suggests that natural selection theory can explain how the family evolved into an emotional unit that exhibits a fundamental conflict between the individual and the group. It would appear from Buss' ideas that for natural selection to explain such an outcome, selection would have had to have acted on the family or social group as well as on the individual. There are some emotional processes in the human family, however, that may not fit easily into current evolutionary theory. A family process that may indicate the need for amplification or modification of evolutionary theory is the regression in functioning and symptom development associated with heightened chronic anxiety. However, before discussing those

Published in Volume 10, No. 3, Summer 1989.

This is a revised version of a paper presented at the Thursday Professional Meeting on July 20, 1989.

aspects of human emotional process that may or may not fit with evolutionary theory, Buss' argument for how natural selection can explain the patterns of embryonic development (ontogeny) will be described. The striking parallels between the developing embryo as an emotional unit and the multigenerational family as an emotional unit stimulated this presentation.

Development is one of the great puzzles of biology. How can the progression from a fertilized egg to a fully formed fetus be explained? Normal development depends on cells dividing the right number of times, growing to the right sizes, migrating to the right places, and differentiating into specialists that are essential for the integrity of the whole. What forces make development an orderly and predictable process? How did the order and predictability come to be? How did the variations in development that produce the vast diversity of life forms evolve? In Buss' book, *The Evolution of Individuality*, the patterns of ontogeny are explained through the application of natural selection theory. It is a pioneering attempt to apply natural selection theory more broadly than it has generally been applied since the modern synthesis (the wedding of population genetics and natural selection theory that occurred early in this century). Buss considers this broader application of natural selection to be more consistent with Darwin's original theory.

Darwin observed that all the offspring of a given organism are not exactly the same, and that these differences among offspring can be passed to their descendants. The existence of heritable variation among offspring means that organisms can evolve to be increasingly suited to their natural habitats. Since the diversity of natural habitats and ecological pressures is great, the diversity of life forms is great. This is the theory of natural selection. The original theory lacked any mechanism by which variation might be inherited. In addition, the original theory envisioned natural selection acting on groups as well as on individuals. In Buss' view a tacit assumption of the modern synthesis is that the individual is the sole unit of biological organization upon which natural selection acts. Buss holds that natural selection can act on may "levels" of biological organization simultaneously. If natural selection is assumed to act on more than one level, and if the conflict between the interest of the component cells of an organism and the interest of the organism as a whole is appreciated, then the evolution of many basic patterns of ontogeny can be explained.

It is generally thought that life originated when certain molecules developed the ability to replicate themselves. Transitions to more complex life forms followed. One theory about the progression to greater complexity is that autonomously replicating molecules were associated into self-replicating complexes, self-replicating complexes were incorporated into cells, autonomously replicating organelles such as mitochondria were also incorporated into cells, cells associated to become multicellular individuals, and individuals associated to become multimember groups. Buss theorizes about one of these transitions or steps towards the development of complex life forms. This transition, which occurred sometime in the Precambrian period, was from free-living, totipotent (undifferentiated) cells to multicellular individuals with division of labor (cell differentiation).

When cells that had been living independently began living in groups, the "group" represented a primitive multicellular organism. At first none of the cells in the group performed any specialized functions. Over time, however, random genetic mutations resulted in some member cells being different from other member cells. If a change in a member cell produced a specialized function (differentiation) that resulted in the total organism being at an advantage relative to other organisms in its ecological niche, natural selection acting at the level of the individual organism would have favored preservation of the new function. It would have favored it because the organism with the advantage would be more likely to survive and reproduce than its less specialized competitors. Since the new function increases the reproductive success of the total organism, it also increases the chances of the member cell specialist's genes being represented in the next generation. The basis of the new function would have to be heritable, but the details of the heritability are too complex for this presentation.

There is a problem, however. When a member cell specializes, it disadvantages its own reproductive potential. By directing its cellular "machinery" to perform a specialized function, it has less machinery available to clone itself. So while the specialist is behaving altruistically (in reference to the organism as a whole) and compromising its own reproduction, its undifferentiated cellular neighbors are behaving individualistically. The individualists preserve their cellular machinery for reproduction and, as a consequence, reproduce faster than the specialist. Herein lies the dilemma. Natural selection acting at the level of the individual organism that has the advantage by virtue of its member cell's specializations favors preservation of that organism. However, natural selection acting at the level of the cell lineages (member cells and their descendants) favors lineages that are producing the most descendants, the undifferentiated lineages. So how did evolution manage to preserve reproductively disadvantaged specialists? Why does the organism not become overrun by undifferentiated cells? Had this overrun occurred, life as we know it would not have evolved.

For a harmoniously functioning, differentiated, multicellular unit (such as *Homo sapiens*) to evolve, mechanisms had to evolve to control the propensity of cells to reproduce without contributing any specialized functions to the group. Natural selection at the level of the individual organism had to effectively oppose selection at the level of cell lineages. Over millions of years the propensity for continued self-replication of cell lineages was in fact (according to this theory) subjugated to the interest of the whole. Buss considers the principal innovation of metazoans (animals having a body composed of cells differentiated into tissues and organs) to be the evolution of processes ("epigenetic controls") that restrain the inherent propensity of cells to self-replicate. The competition between the "rights" of the cell and the "needs" of the group has, through natural selection, achieved a balance that preserves the integrity of the group. This integrity is evident in the orderly patterns of cell division, cell growth, cell migration, and cell differentiation that characterize the development of metazoans.

Buss refers to the controls on cellular self-replication as "epigenetic" because the specialized destiny of any component cell of an organism is not determined by that cell's base sequences of DNA. A cell's outcome is determined, rather, by the interactions between the cell and its environment. The dependence of a cell's outcome on its environment is illustrated by an experiment with an amphibian embryo. For a period in the embryo's development, if cells that would normally develop into an eye are transplanted to other areas of the embryo, the cells will develop into structures appropriate for the area to which they have been transplanted. If the cells are simply cut out of the embryo and allowed to develop in a salt solution, they form no recognizable structures whatsoever. So the cells of an embryo early in development have no capacity on their own to develop into any one structure. Their ultimate fate depends on external influences. These external influences, which are assumed to be encoded in the genomes of other cells, comprise the epigenetic controls.

Several types of epigenetic controls have evolved. One control is *maternal predestination*. When the mother produces an egg, some of her cytoplasm containing messenger-RNA and gene activators is deposited in that egg. This means that after the egg is fertilized, the embryo's own genes do not direct its early development. The mother directs it. No opportunity exists for a cell in the young embryo to "do its own thing." Any increase in selfish individualism is simply not possible. Another important epigenetic control is *induction*. Cells, through electrical or chemical stimuli, can induce neighboring cells to specialize. In response to inductive influences, however, cellular *competence* has also evolved. Competence describes whatever capacity cells have to resist attempts by other cells to dictate to them. Complex interactions during the course of development (consisting of cells pressuring and resisting one another) eventually lead to a developmental outcome of groups of cells differentiated into organs and tissues. The end product appears as a well-integrated, harmonious society of cells, but it actually reflects the restraints evolution has imposed on a fierce underlying struggle between the propensity of cells for self-replication and their capacity for differentiation.

An *interpretation* of Buss' ideas is that natural selection can create an adaptive balance of individual and team play through the development of a multigenerational relationship system. It is not necessary for the genome of any cell lineage to know the "master plan" of the organism. Each cell lineage simply performs functions and behaviors that natural selection has perfected over evolutionary time. A critical component of these functions and behaviors is the way cells interact with other cells. Since the activity of one cell cannot be explained out of the context of its relationship to other cells, the concept of a relationship system is essential. Furthermore, since the characteristics of a cellular relationship system at any given moment depend on the characteristics of earlier generations, the concept of a multigenerational relationship system is also essential.

In family systems theory Bowen describes the influence of the multigenerational relationship system on the emotional functioning and behavior of individual family members. The remarkable orderliness and predictability that characterize human relationship systems are assumed to result from those systems having been shaped by the evolutionary process. Patterns in the relationship system reflect the underlying processes of the emotional system. Family theory describes the interplay between thinking, feeling, and acting for oneself (individuality) and thinking, feeling, and acting under pressure from the relationship system (togetherness). Bowen's discovery (albeit not proven as yet) seems to be an important challenge to evolutionary theorists. The discovery of relationship processes in the human family that are remarkably similar to relationship processes in the developing embryo suggest that the human family or social group is a unit of biological organization upon which natural selection acts. Natural selection having acted on the family as well as on the individual could be what has produced the counterbalancing process ("forces") of individuality and togetherness. (The individuality/togetherness dichotomy is not being precisely equated with the cellular self-replication/cellular differentiation dichotomy.)

What may be another important stimulus to the thinking of evolutionary theorists is the predictable impact of heightened chronic anxiety on relationship systems, an impact consistently observed in human families and social groups. Anxiety can propel a family into an *emotional regression*. In a regression the harmonious balance between individual and team play is undermined. People become both more selfish and more easily led. Relieving the anxiety of the moment increasingly takes precedence over action based on long-range view. Predictable consequences of a protracted regression include relationship disruptions and varying degrees of individual dysfunction. If chronic anxiety diminishes, the regression will reverse. An important point about an emotional regression is that it is the relationship system that is disturbed. Changes in individual functioning are reflections of what is occurring in the larger system. How the phenomenon of emotional regression could possibly be used to amplify or modify evolutionary theory can be illustrated by extending the concept to cancer.

It is generally held that the presence of cancer cells in an organism indicates a primary change having occurred in normal cells that transforms them into cancer cells. Buss reflects this view in stating that cancer cells "succeed because mutations giving rise to them ultimately endow them with a greater replication rate than their neighbors."[1] A transformed cell has the ability to evade normal host controls on its reproduction and to mobilize resources in its environment to support its growth. The question for evolutionary theorists is the following: If cell differentiation during development depends on epigenetic controls, why should such controls not continue to be of paramount influence in adult organisms? Could not the primary disturbance in cancer be a disturbance in the epigenetic controls on cell differentiation? A cell in an adult organism may continue to replicate rather than differentiate because it does not receive the signals from other cells on which its differentiation depends. Cancer may reflect a disturbance or regression in cellular relationships that is fostered by heightened chronic anxiety.

Viewing cancer as primarily reflecting a disturbed balance of cellular relationships appears to extend Buss' ideas about the evolution of developmental processes. The extension is the following: Not only has the evolution of multicellular, cellular differentiated organisms depended on striking a balance between the self-replication propensity of cells and their capacity to become specialists, but the processes that created that balance over evolutionary time continue to be critical to its maintenance. Balance is not fixed in stone, but vulnerable to disintegration. While the processes that maintain balance are encoded in the genomes of cells, since no one cell knows the "master plan" of the organism, it seems appropriate to consider balance an evolved property of the organism as a whole rather than as a property of individual cells. In addition, if the notion of balance is to be included in the theory, the concept of anxiety seems essential for

---

[1] Leo W. Buss. 1987. *The Evolution of Individuality*. Princeton: Princeton University Press.

explaining the predictable, stepwise regressions in organism or group functioning that can occur.

Other intriguing possibilities exist. Could it be that it is the relationship system that evolves? Perhaps this goes without saying, but, traditionally, it has been difficult to conceptualize things this way. People such as Bowen and Buss seem to be making such conceptualizations more plausible. While it is posited that in regression changes in the functioning of members of a group (cellular or family group) reflect changes in the total group, it is also posited that for a group to alter its basic way of doing things, one or more individuals in the group must be innovative. By being innovative, that group member is less in step with (or perhaps more in step with) the group. How a change in a group member is understood to affect the group as a whole depends on whether a group is conceptualized as a "collection of individuals" or as an "emotional unit."

If a group is conceptualized as a collection of individuals, a group member being out of step puts pressure on the group by virtue of his not doing tasks the group has relied on him to do or by virtue of his doing things that somehow interfere with what other group members are doing. The effect of his change is, in a sense, indirect. It is indirect because a collection of individuals are interdependent only by virtue of shared tasks. They are not functionally linked in more profound ways.

In contrast, if a group is conceptualized as an emotional unit, a group member being out of step puts pressure on the group in direct ways. This is because a cardinal feature of an emotional unit is reciprocal functioning. A change in functioning of any one member of the unit results automatically in compensatory changes in functioning of other group members. The automatic nature of the process results from the intricate connections that exist between individuals. Family systems theory describes significant limits on the autonomy of emotional functioning of family members, a lack of autonomy largely mediated by visual and vocal stimuli. Buss describes significant limits on the autonomy of cells, a lack of autonomy largely mediated by chemical and electrical stimuli.

Are Buss and Bowen presenting evidence that the concept of an emotional unit applies on all levels of biological organization? If so, it seems to support the notion that it is the relationship system, not members of the system, that evolves. A change in an emotional system depends on a member of that system functioning or acting differently, but since the member's change would have immediate, direct effects on the group, it would seem appropriate to conceptualize the system as evolving rather than its component parts evolving. The notion that the system evolves parallels ideas proposed in 1917 by Scottish biologist D'Arcy Wentworth Thompson. In a classic work, *On Growth and Form*, Thompson proposed that the evolutionary transformation of one species into another is a process involving the entire organism rather than successive minor alterations in the body parts. Thompson supports his view by demonstrating how the shapes of related species are relatively simple distortions of one another.

The study of cancer seems to be a very important area for attempting to document some of the speculations that have been presented. Cancer appears to reflect a breakdown in what evolution took eons to perfect. All the fundamental processes that have shaped and maintained evolutionary change seem to come into sharp focus in the development of cancer. A principal obstacle to seeing those processes may be a bias about what one should be seeing. Enough may now be known about cancer to put the pieces together, but putting them together may require thinking about "old" facts in a new way.

REFERENCES

D'Arcy W. Thompson. 1917/1952. *On Growth and Form*. Two volumes. London: Cambridge University Press.

BOWEN THEORY AND EVOLUTIONARY THEORY

MICHAEL E. KERR, MD

Many students of Bowen theory have become interested in its relationship to evolutionary theory. This is not surprising in light of Bowen's effort to make his theory consistent with facts about evolution. Over the years, however, people have sometimes talked as if Bowen theory and evolutionary theory can be easily integrated. The two theories draw on many of the same facts about human beings and the rest of the natural world, but the concepts in each theory are sufficiently distinct that it is important not to mix them.

Countless facts about many species lead most thoughtful people to the conclusion that all extant forms are the product of lineages that extend back to the time life first appeared on earth. The complex organisms of today originated in the simplest life processes of three and a half to four billion years ago. Most of the species that have ever existed no longer exist, but life on Earth has continued uninterrupted. The view that changes in successive generations of a multitude of lineages have produced the diversity of life forms is called "evolution." Many people accept evolution as a fact, although perhaps not with the same conviction that they accept the Earth being a sphere as a fact. The creationists, of course, do not believe evolution is a fact.

Darwin used the facts about evolution to develop the theory of natural selection, which attempts to explain how evolution occurs. Simply stated, the species presently inhabiting the Earth are here because the parents of the living members of each species were able to adapt sufficiently to their environments to generate

Published in Volume 13, No. 3, Fall 1992.

enough offspring similar to themselves to replace the parental generation as it died off. The members of the generation preceding the parents were able to do the same thing. Species that have become extinct did so because their members were unable to adapt sufficiently to sustain adequate generativity. Failures in adaptation may be related to changes in the biological or physical environment, or, presumably, to changes in the species itself. Successes in adaptation may be related to particular structural or behavioral innovations certain members of a species develop, or to favorable environmental circumstances. In this way, nature selects which individuals and, consequently, which species, survive. It is thought that new species emerge when some descendants are sufficiently different from their progenitors that they can no longer produce viable offspring from mating with organisms like their progenitors.

Evolutionary theorists, therefore, are interested not only in facts about the anatomy, physiology, and behavior of extinct and living species, but they are interested in understanding the natural selective forces that lead to specific structural and behavioral adaptations. The question they pose is, "What function has a particular anatomical structure or behavior served to make the individual having that structure or behavior more or less adaptive to the environment in which he lived or lives?" In other words, the theorists are interested not only in *what is*, but in how *what is* came to be. The theory of natural selection has been the principal mode for understanding how evolution has take its particular paths. The theory had even been used to predict what kinds of environmental conditions are conducive to certain structures or behaviors evolving. For example, Richard Alexander used natural selection theory to predict the conditions under which a mammal might evolve to have a social organization similar to a eusocial insect colony. The naked mole rat, with its social insect-like organization, was later discovered to live in conditions that matched Alexander's predictions almost perfectly.

Darwin held that natural selection operated on individual members of a species, not on groups of individuals or on the species as a whole. However, he did extend his ideas about how natural selection operates to address the question of how sterile individuals could evolve, as they do in social insects. If these individuals leave no offspring, how can natural selection operate? He eventually dealt with this problem by proposing that selection can operate within the "family." He wrote,

> a breed of cattle, always yielding oxen with extraordinarily long horns, could be slowly formed by carefully watching which individual bulls and cows, when matched, produced oxen with the longest horns; and yet no one ox could ever have propagated its kind.[1]

Darwin was unaware of Mendel's discoveries about genetics, but evolutionary theorists in this century incorporated genetics into their attempts to explain how sterile castes and how altruistic behavior can evolve. Altruism is defined as functioning that enhances the reproductive success of others at the expense of one's own reproductive success. Combining knowledge of genetics with natural selection theory led to the question, "How can genes that are assumed to govern altruistic behavior spread through a population based on natural selection?" For example, how can genes governing the altruistic behaviors of sterile worker ants—who spend their life energies supporting the reproductive efforts of others—be transmitted to the next generation?

Evolutionary theorists have developed several concepts to explain how "altruistic genes" could spread through a population. The most influential concepts are the following: inclusive fitness and kin selection (Hamilton), reciprocal altruism (Trivers),

---

[1] Charles Darwin 1979 [1859]. *On the Origin of Species by Means of Natural Selection.* New York: Avenel Books, pp. 258-259.

parental manipulation (Alexander), and colony selection (Wilson). Some have argued that the evolution of altruism can be explained by natural selection operating at the level of the group or species. Other than Wilson's specific application to social insect colonies, however, most theorists now consider the idea of group selection untenable.

The important point for this discussion is that concepts such as inclusive fitness, kin selection, reciprocal altruism, parental manipulation, and colony selection are part of evolutionary theory, not facts about evolution itself. Given the facts that support evolution having occurred, these concepts represent attempts to explain how evolution has occurred. Each concept is anchored in the assumption that change in an organism's genes (mutations and recombinations) are the principal source of variation on which natural selection acts.

Bowen theory is based on the facts of evolution, not on evolutionary theory. Bowen held that the human family is a system that is governed by laws that govern other natural systems. The concept of the emotional system is the link between *Homo sapiens* and nonhuman species. The human emotional system originated in the "simple" life processes that emerged billions of years ago and through its long lineage has somehow evolved into its present form.

The family relationship system is one way the emotional system manifests itself. Bowen theory may not fit easily into current evolutionary theory. For example, by describing the family as an emotional unit that governs individual behavior and development, Bowen theory introduces a new system of regulation on individual functioning. This family regulatory system may even, over the course of generations as well as in the present, help regulate the functioning of genes. If this view is accurate, it will never be possible to locate genes for schizophrenia in the schizophrenic person. In other words, the genes of every other family member will have to be included in a complete explanation. Bowen theory requires a shift from cause-and-effect thinking (the cause exists within the individual) to systems thinking (the individual regulates and is being regulated by the functioning of others in ways that can be understood only by examining the system as a whole). How such a regulatory system evolved may not be a question that current evolutionary theory can answer. As mentioned, Bowen theory does not attempt to answer this question.

Other phenomena described by Bowen theory may challenge the thinking of evolutionary theorists. For example, the dramatic changes in the functioning of a system that sometimes occur depend on the level of anxiety. Biologists are aware of the impact of anxiety on physiology and behavior in nonhuman species, but the concept of anxiety does not seem very well integrated into the theoretical thinking of biology. Other phenomena described by Bowen theory that may challenge the thinking of evolutionary theorists include the potent tendencies toward fusion and differentiation, the phenomenal predictability of reciprocal functioning, and the automatic mechanisms human beings use to manage the intensity of togetherness that also appear to be used by a wide range of other species, even fairly simple forms of life. Does what Bowen and now many others have observed in the human family and other human groups tap into something quite fundamental in life processes, something that can make dichotomies such as biological versus cultural less relevant?

In addition to thinking about old facts in a new way, Bowen did discover some new facts about emotional functioning by studying human beings. He crafted a new theory to fit with the new facts, one that could incorporate the old facts. As time passes and more and more species are studied, many of the facts Bowen discovered about human relationship systems are being observed in other species. Perhaps the new facts will push evolutionary theorists toward a new way of thinking, toward new theoretical concepts. The new concepts may be more consistent with concepts in Bowen theory than are some of the present concepts in evolutionary theory. For now, it is important to keep the distinctions between Bowen theory and evolutionary theory in focus.

REFERENCES

Alexander, Richard. 1974. "The Evolution of Social Behavior." *Annual Review of Ecological Systems* 5:325-383.

Hamilton, W. D. 1964. "The Genetical Theory of Social Behavior." *Journal of Theoretical Biology* 7:1-52.

Sherman, Paul D., Jennifer U. M. Jarvis, and Richard Alexander. 1991. *The Biology of the Naked Mole-Rat.* Princeton: Princeton University Press.

Trivers, Robert L. 1971. "The Evolution of Reciprocal Altruism." *The Quarterly Review of Biology* 46:35-57.

Wilson, E. O. 1985. "The Sociogenesis of Insect Colonies." *Science* 228:1489-1495

COMPLEX BIOLOGICAL SYSTEMS

MICHAEL E. KERR, MD

A year ago I wrote an article for the Family Center Report entitled, "Bowen Theory and Evolutionary Theory." The article was an attempt to define some distinctions between the two theories. Bowen theory describes the human family as an emotional unit, and it uses systems thinking to deal with the complex, interdependent processes that occur in the unit. Besides describing some specific patterns of emotional functioning present in all families, the theory holds that two basic life forces, differentiation and togetherness, account for variations in the intensity of the patterns. The theory does not address how the human family evolved to function as an emotional unit; it only assumes that it did. In contrast, Darwin's theory attempts to explain how evolution occurs, principally by the process of natural selection. It attempts to explain how human beings and other species have come to look and act the way they do. Whether the forces and patterns described by Bowen theory evolved solely by natural selection is, at this point, an unanswered question.

During the past year, based on continued reading in biology, on discussions with biologists Stephen Emlen and John Bonner, and on exchanges with colleagues in my own field, I have thought more about the relationship between Bowen theory and evolutionary theory. One of the things that has impressed me during my continuing exploration of biology is how well Bowen structured the terms and concepts of his theory to fit with biology. The definitions of some terms such as "emotion" do not fit exactly with common usage in biology, but ideas such as function, functioning position, and facts of functioning fit well with biology.

Published in Volume 14, No. 4, Fall 1993.

When people knowledgeable about Bowen theory first
began to study concepts developed by sociobiologists, some dis-
agreed with the tight links many sociobiologists were making
between genes and behavior. The notion of a gene for altruism
was an example. The sociobiological way of thinking appeared
to collide with observations of human families indicating that
relationships strongly influence the behavior of individuals. The
gene-behavior link implied that internal forces primarily govern
behavior rather than the interplay between internal and external
forces described by Bowen theory.

An important reason for inviting Stephen Emlen to be the
Distinguished Guest Lecturer at last year's Annual Symposium
was that he represented a shift in thinking in sociobiology. Dr.
Emlen had observed that social behaviors are typically highly
flexible in their expression, which implies only a loose link between specific genes and specific behaviors. He was quoted to
say:

> Animals possess a wide variety of options in their behavioral
> repertoire and choose to express those options that yield the
> highest fitness payoffs given the ecological and social circum-
> stances the animal finds itself in.[1]

In other words, an animal might behave altruistically in
one situation but not in another. This way of thinking allows for
an interplay between internal and external forces in determining
behavior. A reason the work of Jack Calhoun has long been of
interest to people knowledgeable about Bowen theory is that he
has consistently emphasized the interplay of relationships and
individual behavior.

The vantage point of Bowen theory is yet another step beyond recognizing an individual's flexibility of response. Besides

---

[1] Quoted in *Mosaic*, National Science Foundation, Vol. 22, No. 1, Spring
1991, p. 15.

describing a flexibility of response by the individuals who comprise an emotional unit, Bowen theory describes two other processes: (1) individual responses function to maintain overall patterns in a group, and (2) overall patterns in a group regulate individual responses. It is not possible to explain adequately an individual's behavior by just examining what function the behavior seems to serve for that individual. A complete explanation depends on viewing the individual in the context of its social or emotional unit.

Studying organisms in the context of their social systems is not new to biology. Social insects, birds, and other species have been studied in this way for years. Darwin was well aware of how individuals in many species are strongly influenced by their social groups. Dr. Calhoun has studied societies of mice, rats, and other species. He has carefully documented how social organization breaks down under certain conditions, how the breakdown affects individuals, and how the effects on individuals further contribute to the breakdown. Bowen's profound insight is that the human family is also a complex biological system. The family exhibits patterns of emotional functioning that appear identical to patterns observed in other species. For example, it appears that all species that live in well-integrated societies exhibit reciprocal functioning between individuals and between groups of individuals.

If cells, insects, and mammals have evolved into social groups that have common patterns of emotional functioning, then debates about the impact of genes versus relationships on individual functioning seem unnecessary and unresolvable. Genetic processes and relationship processes have evolved as an intertwined whole. Even the activities of specific genes are inseparable from the relationships between genes. In his book, *The Evolution of Complexity*, John Bonner describes this intertwining of genes and relationships in species at many levels on the phylogenetic tree. He conceptualizes the intertwining as "somatic complexity." [2]

Somatic complexity refers to a process in which differences among individuals arise through interactions between individuals rather than through direct gene effects. Relationship processes determine differentiation among cells in multicellular organisms, morphological and behavioral differences among castes in social insect colonies, and physiological and behavioral differences among members of societies of birds and mammals. Cells of a multicellular organism (which are genetically identical) and members of the same species (which have most genes in common) have an ability to vary within a certain range that is determined genetically. Differences among individuals in a social group reflect different parts of that range of variation being expressed. A relationship process regulates the specific expressions. The process results in certain signals being sent to certain individuals both during their developmental and mature stages. Direct gene effects could determine some aspects of an animal's behavior, such as degree of aggressiveness, but the animal's position (and associated functioning) in a social group depends on its interaction with fellow group members. For example, all the females in a naked mole rat colony are genetically capable of functioning in the alpha position (thereby being reproductive) but, based on relationships, only one female at a time holds that position.

An important point in the idea of somatic complexity is that genes are essential participants in the functioning of relationship systems (my phrase, not Dr. Bonner's), but the effects of genes are weak and remote. It would be difficult to predict the character of an organism or of a social group by examining

---

[2] John Tyler Bonner. 1988. *The Evolution of Complexity.* Princeton: Princeton University Press.

the sequence of nucleotides in the active genes of group members. This is because there are so many interactions at levels beyond the genes that determine the outcome. This does not imply that the interactions are totally random and out of control. Although some chance interactions occur, the outcome of development in terms of differentiation of parts is amazingly precise in naked mole rat colonies, insect colonies, and embryos. Presumably, natural selection acts on all of the ramifications of every genetic change (resulting from point mutation, recombination, gene jumping, or transformation) to preserve that which makes the individual and the relationship system more adaptive.

A termite colony nicely illustrates the interplay of genes and relationship systems. Like all eusocial insects, termite colonies are composed of castes, with each caste having a predictable percentage of colony members. Natural selection has determined the proportions in each caste that make a colony maximally adaptive to the circumstances in which it exists. Relationship processes create and maintain the correct balance. The role of relationships can be illustrated by removing all the members of the soldier caste from a termite colony. Predictably, the next batch of nymphs preferentially molts into soldiers rather than into a mixture of caste members (to replace those lost by natural attrition). The mechanisms that mediate the replacement of the soldiers are known. Soldier termites secrete a pheromone that regulates the balance of two hormones in the nymphs: juvenile hormone (which activates genes that catalyze the development of workers) and molting hormone (which activates genes that catalyze the development of soldiers). If the soldier-secreted pheromone concentration in the colony decreases (as occurs when the soldiers are removed), molting hormone increases in the nymphs. After enough soldiers have developed, the soldier-secreted pheromone is at a level that favors an increase in juvenile hormone in the nymphs and a reciprocal decrease in molting hormone.

I infer from what is known about the interplay between genes and the relationship system in termite colonies that the development of a nymph into a soldier requires the activation (or inactivation) of genes in individuals other than just the nymph. For this reason, in a sense, there are no "soldier genes" in one individual. The genes in one individual that make the proteins essential for setting processes in motion that create a soldier are regulated by processes that exist outside that individual. The total complex of interactions has evolved, not just those components that exist within one organism. Genes shape the relationship system and the relationship system is a selective force on genes. Thus, genes and relationships are highly intertwined.

The mode for the generational transmission of information in termites appears to be strictly genetic. The genes contain all the information that determines the nature of a termite relationship system. More complex species such as our own transmit information behaviorally as well as genetically. Behavioral transmission involves teaching, learning, and memory. The important distinction is that the capacity to teach, learn, and remember has a genetic basis, but the content of what is taught, remembered, or learned is not encoded in the genes. Since the capacity for behavioral transmission is genetically based, genes ultimately control (control in the sense that the information is encoded in the genes) both the genetic and behavioral transmission of information. However, the connection between the flexible behavior exhibited by complex species (which involves multiple choices and inventiveness) and the genome is even more remote than the connection between termite behavior and the genome.

A remote connection between the genome and flexible behavior does not imply a lack of precision or predictability to a multigenerational process that includes both genetic and behavioral modes of information transmission. The multigenerational transmission process described by Bowen theory includes both genetic and behavioral components, yet the process is "genetic-like" in its precision and predictability. For example, the basic levels of differentiation of children, which result from an interplay between innate processes and life experience, are never markedly different from the basic levels of their parents.

The precision and predictability of a multigenerational process that includes genetic and behavioral components seem to be the consequence of what appears to be a functional interconnection existing between behaviorally and genetically transmitted aspects of relationship systems. The interconnection appears to include the capacity for behaviorally transmitted information to regulate indirectly the activity of at least some genes. Behavioral transmission has evolved in the context of genetically determined aspects of relationship systems, and changes in relationship systems that are based on learning are strong selective forces on genes. Thus, genetic and behavioral transmission are highly intertwined.

Bowen theory refers to complex biological systems as emotional units. Multicellular organisms, eusocial insect colonies (eusocial species have overlapping generations, one or a few reproductives, and many functionally sterile helpers[3]), and naked mole rat colonies are all emotional units. The striking similarity between emotional units that have evolved to these extreme levels of cohesion, cooperation, and altruism[4] suggests that natural selection, at least in part, shapes the characteristics of an emotional unit for a particular species by acting on the unit of

---

[3] These criteria were defined by Michener in "Comparative Social Behavior of Bees," *Annual Review of Entymology*, Vol. 14, 1969, pp. 299-342.

[4] E. O. Wilson, in *Sociobiology: The New Synthesis* (1975) uses these three variables to assess a species' level of sociality.

reproduction of that species. The unit of reproduction in naked mole rat colonies (where on average eighty functionally sterile individuals support a few reproductives) is the colony as a whole. It is very obvious in this mammalian species how individuals function to maintain patterns in the relationship system and how patterns in the system regulate individual development and behavior. The relationship system orchestrates an adaptive mosaic of interacting phenotypes. The system is also a strong selective force for the evolution of extreme adaptations (such as functional sterility) that benefit the individual by being profitable to the community.

Richard Alexander suggests that it was specific environmental conditions that favored the evolution of eusociality in termites, naked mole rats, and other species.[5] It became advantageous for members of these species to live in long-lasting, multigenerational inbreeding groups, probably because it made them safer from predators and improved their ability to garner food resources. The availability of an expandable nest and a food supply requiring minimal risk to obtain it were other factors favoring increasingly integrated group living. Thus, environmental conditions favored the formation of groups and, once formed, intragroup interactions functioned as a selective force for adaptations that enhanced social integration.

The patterns of emotional functioning in the human family have much in common with the patterns in naked mole rat colonies. For example, reciprocal functioning, synchronous behaviors, dominant-subordinate interactions, conflict, distance, and individual alliances to subordinate others characterize both species. However, the unit of reproduction in *Homo sapiens* is dif-

---

[5] A summary of Alexander's ideas are in "The Evolution of Eusociality" Richard D. Alexander, Katherine M. Noonan, and Bernard J. Crespi in *The Biology of the Naked Mole Rat*. Paul W. Sherman, Jennifer U. M. Jarvis and Richard D. Alexander, eds. Princeton University Press, 1991.

ferent from that of our rodent relatives. In our species a father, mother, and children, and often grandparents and other relatives, generally compose the unit of reproduction. In contrast to naked mole rats, the majority of human offspring reproduce by starting reproductive units of their own. If Alexander is correct, the unit of reproduction in our species is different from eusocial species because we evolved in different circumstances.

My hypothesis, and conclusion, from the foregoing data and ideas is that the emotional system of a naked mole rat colony, having evolved based on different units of reproduction, is simply a more extreme version of the human family emotional system. Similar patterns of emotional functioning regulate development and behavior in human beings and naked mole rats, but the process is not so intense in human beings as to have fostered the evolution of most family members being functionally sterile or the evolution of some of the morphological specializations that occur in naked mole rats. In human beings, however, the relationship system profoundly affects the level of adaptive functioning (differentiation) of individuals. This effect on adaptive functioning may occur in naked mole rats as well. That patterns of emotional functioning similar to those in rodents and human beings exist in fish, birds, reptiles, insects, and other classes of organisms raises further questions about how deeply embedded these patterns are in living systems.

Reproduction, Survival and Extinction

Roberta B. Holt, DSW

Introduction

In a search for basic principles that influence the functioning of the human family, this exploration focuses on the processes of reproduction, survival, and extinction. Knowledge about any aspect of how the human functions can make a contribution to a broader understanding of life. A specific examination of the processes of survival and extinction in the human family addresses the question of the essential elements without which a family can and cannot survive. Broadly, this paper seeks to discover some of the basic processes that emerge in families that extinct, while also defining some of the processes that appear to correlate with survival.

The Work of Charles Darwin

Reading the original work of Charles Darwin provides a wealth of information about biology and processes in the natural world. The core of much that Darwin had to say about these processes concerns survival and what Darwin referred to as the "struggle for existence." [1] Most of the observations he made are as accurate now as they were when he first made them in the 1800s.

Darwin considered the group as the important unit for understanding individual behavior. He called this group the colony or the family unit. He arrived at this definition through a series of reasoned steps in observing and thinking about reproductive patterns in animals across a number of species. He observed

Published in Volume 10, No. 4, Fall 1989.

[1] Charles Darwin. [1859] 1958. *The Origin of Species*. New York: New American Library, p. 73.

that, in nature, each individual, with rare exceptions, begins with the equipment for reproduction. But, all individuals with the capacity to reproduce in fact do not do so. Since reproduction does not take place, there have to be important mediators that influence whether the individual organism does or does not reproduce. These influences have to be strong enough to transcend the individual. Focusing on the individual provided few clues to this mystery. By observing patterns of interaction in the colony, Darwin realized that the colony became organized in a dominance hierarchy in which various individuals performed various functions related to the life of the entire unit. He reasoned that the important unit in which reproductive success is determined is in the dominance hierarchy. Knowledge of the organism's position in the colony or family unit, rather than of the individual organism itself, was predictive of reproductive success.

While Darwin originally defined this basic observation about fertility, it was not until the 1960s that the concept was examined more fully, when W. D. Hamilton published his work on what was to become known as altruistic behavior in social animals. Hamilton's research was based on the observation that in social groups of animals there were non-reproducing and neuter individuals who were found to perform tasks in the context of the larger family unit. These tasks contributed to the survival of the family group. This contribution to the unit he called "altruism," [2] and it included not only behavior beneficial for the survival of the social group but, in some instances, beneficial for the individual performing the behavior. For example, across species lines, the adolescents of the species are often found to take care of the young of others in the group. Such behavior provides a service to the group, but also provides an avenue for learning skills necessary in the adolescent's development as a potentially competent parent.

---

[2] W. D. Hamilton. 1964. "The Genetical Theory of Social Behavior, I, II." *Journal of Theoretical Biology* 7:1-52.

In addition to developing ideas about natural selection, Darwin also wrote about what he called the "struggle for existence." Broadly, this struggle for existence was defined as "the dependence of one being on another."[3] The definition included not only the individual, but that individual's success in leaving progeny. In this struggle, he saw the process as being most severe between individuals of the same species, "for they frequent the same districts, require the same food, and are exposed to the same dangers."[4] Those of the same group have similar habits and genetic constitution, further setting the stage for potential conflict.

A key variable in the struggle for existence, in Darwin's view, was whether offspring and progenitor came into what he called "competition."[5] Under such conditions there was a tendency in the descendants of any one species to supplant and exterminate their immediate predecessors and the original progenitor. The exception to this rule occurred when the offspring of a species migrated to a distinct country or became quickly adapted to some new station in which offspring and progenitor were no longer able to compete and both could continue to exist.

In observing the patterns of extinction among various species, Darwin found that it was larger social groups that often developed new varieties or species that were able to perpetuate themselves. He believed these larger biological families already had an advantage in that the largeness of the group demonstrated that the species had inherited from a common ancestor some advantages in common. At the broad level of survival of the species or of society, the struggle for the production of new and modified descendants is seen as occurring within the larger groups. The processes of extinction, however, occurred in the

---

[3] Darwin, p. 75.
[4] Darwin, p. 83.
[5] Darwin, p. 119.

subgroups of these "small and broken" [6] fragments from the larger colony that were the ones to disappear.

THE WORK OF MURRAY BOWEN

Bowen theory addresses neither survival nor extinction in a direct, step-by-step way. However, its concepts are consistent with natural processes and are broad enough to provide useful ideas about conditions necessary for survival and for extinction. The principles of the theory offer avenues for research and exploration of these processes.

Bowen theory defines the unit of observation as the family unit or the system as a whole. In this view the individual, and what he says and feels, is seen as part of the functioning of the emotional system that drives individual behavior. Mediating the impact of the emotionally-driven behavior is the thinking system which has the ability to bring under conscious control many of the aspects of behavior that otherwise would operate at the level of feelings. In this theory, individual behavior influences and is influenced by the thoughts, feelings, and actions in the family unit. How one feels or what one feels is considered to be content. As such, it may or may not provide accurate information about how the broader family system is operating. Generally speaking, the content of the feeling system does not define how family process operates within the group, although feelings can serve as an indicator of the level of intensity and the degree of emotional reactivity to what is occurring in the family. The approach provides a way to transcend feelings about the human condition and anchor observation in the facts of existing natural processes.

Observations made in clinical practice suggest that who the individuals are and the function they perform within the context of the larger family group may have as much to do with

---

[6] Darwin, p. 122.

reproductive functioning as what individuals say about it or how they feel about the subject. In addition, clinical work also provides a database of evidence to suggest that successful reproduction may have as much to do with a relationship between the procreating female and her mother as it does with her relationship with a mate.

One example is selected from many to illustrate. Upon diagnosis of a terminal illness in their mother, three sisters, aged 45, 41, and 36 reproduced within a calendar year. The oldest sister had been married for twenty-three years and had a fifteen-year-old son. Every year since the birth of the son, she had tried unsuccessfully to conceive. The birth of a daughter during the time frame of the mother's diagnosis was considered a miracle. The second sister, the most reproductively fertile member of the siblings, during the corresponding period of time, had completed her family with three children and was not interested in having more. Believing herself no longer able to conceive, she was somewhat shocked to discover that a fourth child would be entering the family. The youngest sister had experienced a number of unsuccessful relationships with men. She married at the age of 35 and produced a son eight months after her marriage and within the calendar year of her mother's diagnosis. In addition to this example, clinical practice provides enough reports of a change in basic functioning in relationship to one's own mother, followed by reproduction shortly thereafter to substantiate that reproductive functioning in the human is not only grounded in the relationship between the procreating couple, but in the relationship of each to their own nuclear families. While it is fact that such phenomena exist, how the process operates is not known. The question is a rich one for further clinical investigation.

There is evidence to suggest that not only patterns of reproduction, but questions of survival and extinction are determined at the level of the broader family unit. Research conducted in the 1970s on families that extincted suggested these units contained patterns of dysfunction and serious cutoff from the larger family units. The findings are consistent with Darwin's earlier observation that extincting branches of families were the subgroups descended from "small and broken" fragments of the larger family system.

The concept of emotional cutoff is of particular importance in observing patterns of survival and extinction. A cutoff is created when the emotional intensity between two individuals in a system becomes sufficiently high that one or both parties distances emotionally from the other and no longer engages the other. As such, the cutoff is a mechanism for dealing with intense emotionality that cannot be contained within the existing person-to-person relationship between two individuals. It usually occurs in the presence of interlocking triangles that respond to the basic disharmony in the original person-to-person relationship.

Bowen theory not only identifies natural processes that occur in the development of a cutoff but goes a step further to define the conditions necessary to bridge a cutoff. The details of the concept of cutoff can be found in Bowen's original work. For purposes of this discussion of survival and extinction, the following ideas taken from clinical practice and research are proposed.

While Darwin defined the struggle for existence as grounded in the dependence of one individual on another, and believed that the key to the struggle was competition between the generations, this author believes Darwin was observing the result of a reaction to a process within a family system or colony, not the actual process itself. Bowen theory provides a more refined lens for viewing the actual process, and has explicated the nature of the interdependence which may or may not lead to cutoff between the generations. Some of the components of the interdependence are the degree of attachment between mother and offspring, the basic and functional levels of differentiation of the family, and the relationship of each child in the basic triangle with parents. These components interacting together contribute to the extent to which cutoff as a mechanism becomes necessary for the survival and integrity of the organism. The higher the level of anxiety in the family unit, the more likely cutoff will occur. Conversely, the more families are able to function calmly, the less likelihood of cutoff.

Central to the management of a cutoff is the concept of differentiation of self. This concept is not about postures or gestures, but about thought and action that goes into the definition of boundaries between self and others in a family system. The act of defining boundaries between past and future generations, if viewed from the perspective of both Darwin and Bowen, is an important component of survival, not only in the psychic sense, but in the physical sense as well. Darwin's idea that extinction occurs in subgroups that descend from small and broken fragments of larger family units suggests that mechanisms that negate the necessity for the split are important. Differentiation of self, with clearer boundaries being established between the past and the present generations, provides a framework for dealing with what Darwin saw as "competition" and which this author sees as reciprocal needs between parents and offspring that bind the child to the parental generation in ways that cutoff becomes the only viable alternative to the emotional intensity. Indirectly, then, the differentiation of self becomes a mechanism for dealing with the potential of competition between offspring and progenitor. It eliminates the need for offspring to migrate to another district and defines in more detail the process that Darwin recognized as a requisite for survival of multiple generations of organisms within the same territory.

Challenging Assumptions

Michael E. Kerr, MD

Bowen family systems theory challenges several commonly held assumptions about the nature of man and the forces that govern human behavior. This challenging of assumptions accounts, I believe, for much of the theory's slow acceptance. Bowen theory is not well accepted for other reasons as well. It is too new for its existence to be widely known. Like any theory, it is unproven. However these reasons do not account for the many people who become acquainted with Bowen theory but do not pursue it, nor do they account for the passion with which some reject and even assail the theory.

One assumption Bowen theory challenges is that the evolution of man's large and highly developed cerebral cortex, which has spawned language, a complex psychology, and an elaborate culture, has resulted in most human behavior not being governed by the instinctual forces that govern the behavior of other species. Thus, human behavior is regarded as a special case in nature. Statements such as, "Human beings have free will; they are not restricted by the determinism that governs other species," reflect this assumption. Bowen theory, in contrast, assumes that the same forces that govern the behavior of other species govern human behavior. The human's ability to think and communicate are quantum leaps beyond the capabilities of other organisms, but these and other more recently evolved brain functions seem often to operate more in the service of elaborating ancient patterns of emotional functioning rather than fundamentally altering those patterns.

Published in Volume 15, No. 3, Fall 1994.

About ten years ago, Murray Bowen and I attended an award ceremony at the National Zoo for noted sociobiologist, E. O. Wilson. This was a few years after the furor had peaked over some of Wilson's writings and public statements that emphasized a biological basis for human behavior. The man who presented the award, who was also a biologist, introduced Wilson by saying, something to the effect, "Many of us in biology do not agree with Ed Wilson's notion that genetic determinism plays a significant role in human behavior; we like to think there is a place for free will." At that moment, Bowen leaned towards me and whispered loudly, "Of course there's a place for free will—differentiation of self!"

I gained more appreciation that evening for the difficulty many people meet with if they try to think about human behavior in evolutionary terms. The difficulty was evident recently in some responses to a *Time* magazine article about marital infidelity. The article made many references to animal research and implied that understanding the behavior of other species may be relevant to understanding human behavior. Some of the negative reactions to this inference were comments such as, "Drawing parallels between human and animal behaviors, particularly problematic behaviors such as violence or infidelity, will be used to justify those behaviors on the basis of people being compelled by their genes. This attitude is wrong because people are different from animals!"

Over the past two decades or so, television programs and popular magazines have increasingly presented material from animal research. A background (and occasionally foreground) implication of these programs and articles has been that animal research may be relevant for better understanding human behavior. While the level of exposure to such research has increased, polarized responses to its implications are still common. The polarization seems again to be a product of dichotomizing between biological determinism and free will. The dichotomy fuels, at least in part, the need to maintain the assumption that man is a unique case in nature. The dichotomy fosters an often unbridled emphasis in some academic circles on human behavior being far more influenced by psychology and culture than by biology. Attitudes may be slowly changing, but it seems that people must get beyond this dichotomy if they are to challenge seriously the assumption that the forces governing human behavior are fundamentally different from the forces governing the behavior of other species.

The concept of differentiation of self bridges the biological determinism-free will dichotomy. It does so by describing how people act more automatically (biologically determined) in some situations than they do in others. Furthermore, people differ in the extent to which automatic behaviors dictate their overall life courses. Acting based on instinctive reactivity may be wholly appropriate and even lifesaving in some circumstances. However, it is also true that the more chronically anxious and unsure of oneself a person is, the more emotional reactivity and subjectivity govern one's actions; in contrast, the calmer and more certain of oneself a person is, the less reactivity floods one's perceptions, which permits more objectivity about one's internal and external worlds. A more realistic view of oneself and of one's environment permits more thoughtful, appropriate, and flexible (free will) responses to life situations. Thus, the concept of differentiation describes human behavior in evolutionary terms without discounting the importance of higher brain functioning.

Differentiation of self did not emerge *de novo* with the evolution of *Homo sapiens*. The "self" has instinctive components as well as learned ones. An interplay or integration exists between all the elements. Bowen describes this in the following way:

> The "self" is composed of constitutional, physical, physiological, biological, genetic and cellular reactivity factors, as they

move in unison with psychological factors. On a simple level, it is composed of the confluence of more fixed personality factors as they move in unison with rapidly moving psychological states. Each factor influences the other and is influenced by the others. The psychological is the easiest to be influenced by the individual.[1]

A second assumption that Bowen theory challenges is the following: human beings are largely autonomous in their emotional functioning. This assumption manifests itself in two attitudes. The first attitude is that people can will themselves to make their nuclear family different from the family they grew up in. This usually means that the person is going to do a better job raising his children than he thinks his parents did raising him. The implication is that his new family will avoid the problems of the family of origin. The second attitude reflecting the assumption of emotional autonomy is people do not view themselves as playing a significant part in the problems developed by those closest to them. A corollary to this attitude is people not seeing the part others play in problems they themselves develop. In other words, emotional autonomy implies that relationships are unimportant in the creation and maintenance of physical, emotional, and social dysfunctions.

Bowen theory describes a profound interdependence in human emotional functioning. Relationships, particularly family relationships, significantly affect how people function in life. Seeing the part people play in one another's problems is not about blame and self-blame. Blame and self-blame are attitudes connected to feelings such as anger and guilt. A factual view of human emotional systems shows that blame and self-blame are linked to a narrow, cause-and-effect perspective. The late Lewis

---

[1] Michael E. Kerr and Murray Bowen. 1988. *Family Evaluation: An Approach Based on Bowen Theory*. New York: W. W. Norton & Company, p. 342.

Thomas expressed his view of man's social interdependence in the following way:

> From earliest infancy on, we can smile and laugh without tak-
> ing lessons, we recognize faces and facial expressions, and
> we hanker for friends and company. It goes too far to say we
> have genes for liking each other, but we tend in that direction
> because of being a biologically social species. I am sure of
> that point: we are more compulsively social, more interde-
> pendent and more inextricably attached to each other than any
> of the celebrated social insects. We are not, I fear, even mar-
> ginally so committed to altruism as a way of life as the bees or
> ants, but at least we are able to sense, instinctively, certain
> obligations to one another.[2]

Bowen theory does not hold that human relationships cause schizophrenia, depression, cancer, multiple sclerosis, shoplift-ing, or violence, but it holds that the emotionally governed rela-tionship environment is usually as essential to the occurrence of such outcomes as other factors such as genes, viruses, diet, and toxic chemicals. Relationships can enhance or undermine an individual's functioning. Paradoxically, many people anxiously resist accepting such a deep level of human interdependence, yet people seem less anxious when they begin to comprehend it.

A third assumption that Bowen theory challenges is the following: it is not possible to develop a science of human be-havior. Historically, people have held this assumption for differ-ent reasons, but a reason that is popular currently, particularly in the mental health field, is that reality is what individuals per-ceive it to be. An extreme version of this view is that there is no reality beyond perception. It is pointless to talk about objectivity

---

[2] Lewis Thomas. 1992. *The Fragile Species.* New York: Charles Scribner's Sons, p. 26.

since people can only define how they see the world, can only define their biases. It is important to define one's biases because they dictate behavior. This view of reality is seductive because biases clearly do have an enormous impact on behavior. Furthermore, how can one ever know if he is really being objective?

Bowen theory rests on an assumption that an observer can be factual (objective) about emotional process, even if he is a participant in the process. Participation with objectivity is possible because people can be "in contact" with an emotional system and remain "outside" the system, at least to some degree. An observer's ability to distinguish his feelings and subjectivity from his thinking makes it possible to be in contact with and still "outside" the system. Such observers can collect facts about emotional functioning and use the facts to formulate a theory. If a theory rests on facts rather than on bias, it will have predictive value and be capable of being disproven.

To seriously engage Bowen theory, people must decide if they think an impersonal (unbiased) theory about human behavior is possible. Facts about the physical world gradually led to the development of an impersonal theory that took mankind to the moon and back. Subjectivity had dominated human thinking about the solar system for centuries, but eventually a theory devoid of subjectivity successfully guided our technology into space. Is it possible to observe facts of functioning about human behavior and use them as the basis of a scientific theory? At this point in our knowledge, neither a "yes" or "no" answer to this question can be proven or disproven, but where people stand on the question (as is the case with the other assumptions Bowen theory challenges) affects how they respond to Bowen theory.

THE BORDERLINE FAMILY

MICHAEL E. KERR, MD

It could be legitimately argued that human evolution began ten to twenty billion years ago with the cosmic big bang. At
least this is the best theory we have. Our solar system took shape
about four and a half billion years ago and the first life on Earth
appeared over three billion years ago. Within the last few weeks,
our orbiting telescope has provided suggestive evidence of at least
fifty other stars, suns similar to our own, that may have solar
systems around them in various stages of development. I believe that life will likely emerge or already has emerged in some
of these newly discovered young solar systems. I believe this to
be likely because I believe that all that exists throughout the universe is governed by natural forces. I do not consider it acciden-
tal, for example, that life evolved on Earth. I think, given suitable
conditions, that life on Earth was probably the inevitable consequence of the action of these forces that govern the universe.

Entities in nature appear to have an affinity for one another. The galaxies and solar systems appear to have formed on
the basis of that affinity. It has been and continues to be an orderly process. The clumpings of matter created by this affinity
seem to lead to the development of greater complexity. Simple
molecules cluster to form more complex molecules. Complex

Published in Volume 6, No. 2, Spring 1984.

*This paper was presented at a symposium on borderline personality disor-
ders held on November 18, 1983 at the V. A. Medical Center in Coatesville,
Pennsylvania. I was invited to participate by Dr. Henry Lederer, my first
teacher in psychiatry in 1962 when I was a freshman medical student at
Georgetown. I consider the topic in a very broad context and concentrate
on the ways that families that generate a borderline personality are much
like all families and much like your family and mine. —M.E.K.*

molecules cluster to form still more complex ones. Random events may play some role in this process of evolving complexity, but it appears to be a much more orderly and predictable process than is accounted for by random events. At some level of complexity, what we have come to call "life" appears. These small particles of life seem to have some kind of attraction for each other, an attraction people like Lewis Thomas have referred to as a symbiotic force in nature. When enough of the small elements have been united, then that natural phenomenon called the cell emerges.

What a wonder of nature! But it was only a beginning, only the bricks from which enormously complex organisms were eventually built. Eventually came the fish, the reptiles, the birds, and the mammals. In time, a mammal finally emerged with the capacity to study the ten to twenty billion years that preceded his development. This mammal, of course, is *Homo sapiens.*

Everyone here today had his "beginning" more than ten billion years ago. Particles in our bodies are probably five to ten billion years old. Nature discards nothing. It was recycling long before man could spell the word.

We humans are a product of evolution, a part of nature. I believe this to be so regardless of what we say to the contrary, and throughout history we have said a great deal to the contrary. Humankind seems always to have wanted to see itself as other than it is. We are still much this way, although the sheer weight of scientific knowledge seems to be gaining on us. The "ultimate" understanding of the human and human behavior will be anchored in an understanding of the forces that govern all natural systems, of all systems that exist throughout the cosmos. Man can achieve this understanding, I believe.

As early as 300–400 BC, more than two thousand years ago, the Greeks proposed that man was not the center of the universe. A number of them believed that the Earth revolved around the sun and that complex life forms had evolved out of the primordial ooze. These thinkers were "proved" wrong and their ideas were buried for two thousand years or so until people like Copernicus, Newton, and Darwin rediscovered them. What took us so long? What is at stake that the human persists in seeing only what he "wants" to see? It was the nature of man, but not all men. It still is the nature of man, but not all men. The people who "proved" the Greeks "wrong" were no different than we are— no smarter, no dumber.

Isaac Newton gave us the first scientific theory. His theory of universal gravitation is a systems theory, at least in a general sense. People like Copernicus and Johannes Kepler provided a detailed description of the motions of the planets, but their work was descriptive and could not *account for* what was observed. Kepler knew exactly where Mars would be on any given day in any given year, but he could not account for why it was always where it was supposed to be. Newton provided the way for accounting for the motions of the planets with his theory of universal gravitation. Newton's theory could predict everything Kepler had observed and much more. Newton was able to deduce all the laws Kepler had worked so long to define. That is the value of theory.

In the years since Newton, the physical sciences have come a long way indeed. Some physicists believe they are on the verge of a *unified field theory*. All physical phenomena would be explained by the interrelationship of four basic forces: gravity, electromagnetic force, strong force, and weak force. Maybe the physicists are not as close as some may think, but it is clear that they are very far ahead of the life sciences.

We have barely begun to conceptualize a theory in the life sciences. Biology remains largely descriptive, albeit with a rapidly developing sophistication in this regard. Concepts about human behavior are also mostly descriptive and often strongly laced with subjectivity. We demonstrate against war and we could just as easily demonstrate against schizophrenia. Our understanding of both phenomena is terribly limited and, as a consequence, genes, chemicals, and certain people get blamed for them.

Interest in the family as it relates to mental illness has existed for a long time and in a variety of disciplines. What has come to be known as the family movement in psychiatry began in the late 1940s and early 1950s. It has been recognized on a national level since about 1957. Many of the early researchers focused on families with a schizophrenic member, but circumstances dictated that as much as anything else. Families in which any type of serious symptom existed could have just as profitably been studied. The extremes of criminal behavior, alcoholism, physical illness, eating disorders, and other problems would have been fair game. A new theory of human behavior with the potential of replacing or subsuming all existing theories of human behavior emerged from family research. This theory was eventually called *family systems theory* or, as I like to call it, the theory of family emotional systems. The man who has gone farthest in developing this theory is Murray Bowen.

What most people tend to think emerged from the study of the family is a new treatment modality called *family therapy*. Family therapy is but a tiny tip of the iceberg that was generated by family research. The largest part of the iceberg and the part still underwater in most people's eyes is family theory.

Family systems theory is built on the premise that man is a product of evolution and remains an integral part of nature. It evolved from the study of the human family and not from general systems theory. It defines mental illness as a product of the part of man common to all other forms of life. To convey the deeper phylogenetic roots of mental illness, the term mental illness was discarded in favor of "emotional illness." The term emotional, in other words, is considered appropriately applied to the behavior of whales, horses, ants, and mice, as well as man. Emotion is not synonymous with feelings; feelings are a much more recent evolutionary acquisition. In the development of family systems theory a most important effort was made to try to keep concepts consistent with ideas from natural systems. By keeping the theory open to new knowledge from other scientific disciplines, it was anticipated that family systems theory could eventually be integrated with systems concepts developed from the study of other natural systems.

Prior to Freud, mental illness was generally considered to be the product of *structural* defects in the brain. Freud's proposal of *functional* disturbances in the brain based on childhood experiences was a bold leap. Today, there is a great deal of interest in biochemical disturbances or defects that may "cause" mental illness. What all these viewpoints have in common is that they seek the primary cause of the problem within the individual.

What intrigued family researchers were relationships. The thinking, feeling, and behavioral chain reactions that occurred within families became the focus of study. Like Johannes Kepler, most people in the family field have stayed on a descriptive level. In attempting to account for what they saw, they would fall back on individual psychodynamics or some other kind of motivating force which had been conceived from the study of individual patients. Bowen took a distinctly "Newtonian-like" step when he developed the concept of an emotional system to account for what could be observed in families. The human family was seen to be governed by natural life forces akin to those that operated throughout nature. Bowen's assertion that the human family is governed by an emotional system was supported by enough evidence to satisfy Bowen to build a theory on it. Accumulated evidence since then in fields like evolutionary biology and in Paul MacLean's research on brain evolution has increased the level of certainty about Bowen's initial conceptualizations.

Family systems theory posits the existence of two counterbalancing life forces: *individuality* and *togetherness*. These forces are assumed to have an instinctual-emotional base. Complexity increases in advancing stages of evolution. In the human, for example, there are interrelated biological, psychological, and sociological components to both individuality and togetherness. Individuality refers to the capacity to be autonomous, to function as a separate individual. Togetherness refers to the affinity people have for each other and is manifested in people's felt need for emotional closeness and their intolerance of difference.

Differentiation is a concept developed to describe the way the forces of individuality and togetherness are managed within the person and within a relationship system such as the family. There are differences between people and between family units in regards to differentiation. These differences are related to the particular balance of those forces characteristic of a given person or family. These differences are "deep" in the sense that they are bred in families over the span of many generations. Alterations in the individuality-togetherness balance are the product of a continually evolving and shifting process that can be fairly easily traced through the multigenerational history of a family. The result in the present generation is fine gradations of difference between people and families in regards to their "level" of differentiation. People fall somewhere on a continuum of differentiation which renders the concept of "normal" of little value in systems theory.

Now let me approach the individuality-togetherness concept in two somewhat related ways in an attempt to clarify it. The first way has to do with the validity of viewing *the family as an emotional unit* rather than as *a collection of individuals*. The family is an emotional system. It operates in such a way that the thinking, feelings and behavior of each member of that family are regulated and directed by the system. Differentiation refers to the fact that this regulatory process is more intense in some families than in others. One can think in terms of a continuum ranging from reasonably well differentiated families to very poorly differentiated or undifferentiated families. The more the undifferentiation of a family, the more the emotional system regulates the very being of each member. Another element to be considered when evaluating the intensity of this emotional regulatory process in a family is the level of chronic anxiety that prevails. The higher the level of chronic anxiety, the more the system is pushed toward greater degrees of undifferentiation. When the chronic anxiety level decreases, the system returns to its baseline level of differentiation.

A second way to think about the individuality-togetherness concept has to do with the potential dilemma posed by relationships in which people have some degree of emotional investment in each other. Systems theory posits that people who marry have equivalent basic levels of differentiation. The capacity of each person to dysfunction as an individual is the same, and the togetherness needs of each person are the same. Basic levels of differentiation are the same regardless of appearances that sometimes seem to belie that fact. Since people's level of differentiation varies, marriages are not the same in terms of the mix of individuality and togetherness that characterizes them. The more undifferentiated the marital relationship, the more it is balanced toward togetherness. The greater the undifferentiation in a marriage, the greater the potential for problems. Another way of saying this is that the more undifferentiated a marital relationship is, the less adaptive it is to stress.

How to understand this diminished adaptiveness? What I have to say about that is oversimplified, but I will do it to make a point. The more the emotionally determined togetherness needs of people in a marriage, the more emotionally interdependent their functioning. People have strong needs for a sense of connection with each other and strong needs for each other to think, feel, and behave in ways that will satisfy the needs of oneself. People need each other and at the same time are prone to feel a pressure and threat from each other. Therefore, the greater the undifferentiation in a marriage, the more potential for chronic anxiety to be generated by the basic nature of the relationship itself. There is the chronic threat of not enough involvement and the chronic threat of too much involvement such that one will be taken over, smothered, or diminished by the other. Not infrequently, people will play out the opposite sides of this dichotomy in a marriage. At extremes, this dilemma becomes unsolvable and leads to a "you die" or "I die" situation. Relationships can be that powerful.

Short of the extremes, what do people characteristically do to manage this dilemma? Family systems theory has defined four mechanisms that are related to the chronic anxiety generated by the dilemma just described. Most nuclear family units manifest some of all four of these mechanisms to be described. Many nuclear families use predominantly one or two "anxiety binding mechanisms."

The most obvious mechanism and perhaps easiest to understand is *emotional distance.* The anxiety generated by the undifferentiation is bound in the distance. It is a compromise. People withdraw physically or withdraw by means of psychological mechanisms, and the anxiety generated by their interaction disappears. The anxiety is bound in that sense. A second mechanism is *marital conflict.* Conflict provides a form of contact and distance at one and the same time. The undifferentiation of each person is externalized into their patterns of interaction. While such externalization undermines cooperation and communication, it can act in the service of preserving the physical and emotional integrity of each person. A third mechanism is one spouse overriding the other. This is a complex mechanism and there is little time here to detail it. It is usually characterized by *reciprocal functioning* such as the following: overadequate-inadequate, strong-weak, decision maker-nondecision maker, and overfunctioner-underfunctioner. This mechanism, taken toward the extremes, can contribute to clinical impairment in one spouse that can be manifested in physical illness, emotional illness, or social dysfunction.

A fourth mechanism to be described is the one most relevant to the development of a borderline personality. The mechanism is not unique to the clinical entity. In this fourth situation, *the undifferentiation of the parents is played out in relationship to a particular child.* The child is an equal participant in the process. This most involved child will grow up with a level of differentiation slightly less than the parents. His life is more intensely regulated by his internal emotional reactions and the harmony of the emotional environment that surrounds him. The siblings of this child are a little freer to grow up "outside" the emotional problem of the family and typically achieve a level of differentiation equal to or slightly better than the parents. The greater the undifferentiation in a nuclear family to be absorbed or bound, the greater the possibility it will involve several children to a significant degree. One child may eventually collapse into schizophrenia, a second may be best characterized as a borderline personality, a third may be seriously hampered by chronic physical illness, and a fourth may be an amazingly "free spirit." This "free spirit" is closely involved with the family, but the family emotional problem did not rub off on him very much. Such a child will be more adaptive than his or her siblings and has, therefore, more likelihood of a stable life course.

Given this perspective just described, focus on distinct clinical entities is replaced by focus on the "background" level of differentiation. Psychosis, borderline personality, and neurosis are not separate compartments, but are graded variations of a common underlying emotional process. In this sense, these clinical entities are symptoms, not diseases.

I do want to put in a word of caution. The family emotional system is not the "cause" of any clinical problem. The emotional system is an extremely important variable for understanding symptom development, but to view it independently of other variables is to lose a systems perspective. There are biological facts, psychological facts, and sociological facts that have been defined as relevant to the origin of schizophrenia, manic-depression, borderline personality, delinquent behavior, and physical illness. In addition, there are facts relevant to all of these clinical entities that have been established from the study of the family emotional system. Family systems theory is only a beginning step for understanding the human family. The theory is open to but does not yet incorporate these other variables. One day we will have a systems theory that does incorporate all of them. One day we will have a scientifically based systems theory about *Homo sapiens* that can be easily integrated with knowledge from the rest of the life sciences. Maybe even more than that is possible. Perhaps a broad theory that incorporates all phenomena in the cosmos and is firmly grounded in scientific observations can be developed.

I have not concentrated on therapy in this presentation, because therapy is so much a product of the way the therapist thinks about the problem. When family concepts are taught as primarily representing a new method of therapy, trainees tend to quickly bypass the fact that family is, most importantly, a new way of thinking. Trainees are quick to append therapeutic techniques onto their preexisting views of the nature of human problems. My main goal here today, in contrast, has been to present these new family ideas in a way that might make it easier to hear them as a new theory. Training therapists is dependent on defining and challenging their basic assumptions about human behavior and not on teaching them a set of techniques. The goal is for all of us to examine the nature of the lens we use to view the world. For the most part, when viewing the human process, this lens has been fashioned far more out of subjectivity than objectivity.

REFERENCES

Thomas, Lewis. 1974. *The Lives of a Cell*. New York: The Viking Press, Inc.

THEORY AND THERAPY

MICHAEL E. KERR, MD

Within the mental health disciplines there has traditionally been an uneasy relationship between *researchers* and *clinicians*. The gap between these groups seems to result, in part, from therapy being generally regarded as an art and research as a scientific pursuit. Furthermore, theory seems to be an abstract notion to many mental health professionals, something of academic interest rather than of practical value. Family systems theory, in contrast, views research, theory development, and the applications of theory as inextricably bound.

Kurt Lewin is purported to have said, "If you want truly to understand something, try to change it." His comment implies that therapy can be a form of research. For example, people learn about differentiation not so much by reading about it, but by trying to function with more of it. Bowen wrote that in his family research project at the National Institute of Mental Health, changes that occurred during family therapy led to theoretical insights such as the concept of the functioning of one person being related to another. This functional interdependence was not obvious until one family member was able to improve his functioning and the change profoundly affected the functioning of other family members. Biologists frequently do similar experiments, albeit in a different way. For example, by removing all the soldier caste members of a termite colony it became possible to observe that a colony is able to respond to this functional void by stimulating members of its larval brood to differentiate exclusively into soldiers. The pheromonal mechanisms that mediate this process were subsequently discovered.

Published in Volume 16, No. 1, Spring 1995.
Reprinted from Family Systems, *Volume 1, No. 2, Fall/Winter 1994.*

Therapy informs theory and theory informs therapy. How theory informs or guides therapy is difficult for many therapists to grasp. Bowen began with a premise that a science of human behavior could be developed. This science could be the basis for the conduct of therapy. Therapy would probably always be an art to some degree, but it could be firmly anchored in principles derived from a factually based theory. One such principle Bowen outlined at NIMH was to make changes in therapy based only on theory, not on clinical judgments or feelings. Heightened anxiety too easily distorts clinical judgment and feelings. Theory, in contrast, is a reliable map for the process of therapy.

Efforts to change can also be a test for a theory's accuracy. Bowen expresses this view in the following statement made after a successful effort to manage himself differently in his family: "To me the most important long-term accomplishment was the proof that an emotional system has a knowable structure and function, and that one can work out predictable answers on a drawing board." An implication of this view is that if a family fails to make progress, the obstacle may be more in the way the therapist thinks about the family's problem rather than in the family's capacity to change.

Another reason for trying to maintain a balance between theory, research, and applications of theory is that family systems theory addresses the full range of human emotional functioning. Bowen commented that one of the reasons it was possible for him to see the family as an emotional unit was that he studied families with fairly extreme problems such as chronic schizophrenia and severe alcoholism. The interdependence of emotional functioning between family members is more easily observed in such families. Further research showed, however, that the patterns of family interaction that underlie severe symptoms are present in all families, but the patterns are less intense in families with less severe symptoms and less intense still in high functioning families. This led to the concept of the *scale of differentiation* which places the full range of human emotional functioning on a continuum. Differences between individuals and families are quantitative rather than qualitative. Society's best functioning people are a product of the same basic emotional forces that produce society's most impaired people.

Family research's window on the emotional system then was the study of severe clinical problems. Once the emotional system was recognized, it was seen to operate not only in all families, but also in small non-family groups, large organizations, whole societies, and in other species. Although not yet extensively studied, there is evidence that clinical symptoms in members of other species are often connected to the emotional system that operates in their social unit. If further animal research confirms this link between symptoms and the relationship system, it will further establish a remarkable consistency between human emotional functioning and the emotional functioning of other forms of life.

THEORY

&

PRACTICE

Psychotherapy—Past, Present and Future

Murray Bowen, MD

REVIEWED BY

Michael E. Kerr, MD

Dr. Bowen began his presentation by discussing some of the early antecedents of "talking therapy." The earliest were the egg-laying reptilian mothers who showed some interest in protecting their young. The existence of instinctual processes that govern the pattern of relationships between parents and young in many subhuman species contradict the notion that family relationships were developed by the human family. In addition, sociobiologists such as E. O. Wilson have demonstrated that altruism, an important component of the social process, is not confined to the human species.

The most dramatic change during man's several million year evolution has been the explosive growth of the brain. Paul MacLean has shown that man's brain is really three brains, a "triune" brain. The R-complex and limbic system are two portions of the human brain that developed as evolution proceeded through reptiles and early mammals. In man, these parts of the brain perform many of the same functions they do in lower animals. The large neocortex and its prefrontal lobes are unique to man and allow him to think, reason, and reflect. The evolution

Published in Volume 7, No. 3, Summer 1986.

Dr. Bowen's presentation at the Thursday Professional Meeting in February, 1986 was based on a formal paper he had delivered at the "Evolution of Psychotherapy Conference" in Phoenix in December 1985. The presentation was a review of some of the important changes that have marked the development of psychotherapy, and some "educated guesses" about the future direction of the profession.

of man and his culture, however, are but a tiny fragment of the long history of life on the planet. Primitive civilization is only about 30,000 years old.

With his developing brain, man has been able to define the fact that his brain, skeleton, muscles, lungs, digestive tracts, and internal organs are similar to subhuman life forms. He is structurally related to all life. With his brain, he has been able to comprehend the rhythm of the universe, the solar system, the earth, the seasons, the tides, and the weather. We now know that these are all interlocking systems comprising a giant explainable and predictable natural system.

The cerebral cortex has produced the accepted sciences which can be measured, validated, proven, and predicted. At the opposite end of the spectrum are the arts, made up of feelings, subjectivity, impressions, imagination, and ideas that can neither be validated nor proven. There are also disciplines in the midground such as biology—almost a science, but not quite. Medicine contains elements of science and art. Psychiatry, psychology, anthropology, and sociology are clearly in the arena of the non-sciences.

Early on in his professional life, Bowen wondered what it would take to elevate Freudian theory to a scientific level. Psychoanalytic theory contained numerous elements of subjectivity—thinking impressions and ideas from literature. None could be proven according to the principles of science. It was not until Bowen began full-time family research in 1954 that he found some missing links that pointed toward a direction for making concepts about human behavior into a science. The background orientation for the development of a new theory included the following: a strict view of the human as an evolutionary creature, the use of a natural systems theory based on all forms of life, and the recording of facts that could be validated. A new theory was evident by 1956, but Bowen believed it could not be accepted as a science for at least a century. At that time he believed, "If evolution is ever accepted as a scientific theory, then human behavior will also become an accepted scientific theory." Bowen still believes this.

Through the centuries there has been a lag time between the introduction of an idea and its general acceptance. The closer a scientific idea gets to man himself, the more vigorous the opposition to its acceptance. Through reactivity, feelings, religion, superstition, imagination, and limited access to scientific fact, the human has created tremendous distortions that go into the spiritual world. Primitive medicine men believed that illness was caused by evil spirits, and good treatment was ritual to drive out the evil spirits. Witchcraft existed for several hundred years. "We can look with horror at the misassumptions of the past, and hope that such actions are behind us, but the human is still human, the potential for wild imagination is alive and well, and we are always vulnerable to righteous action based on misassumption," said Bowen.

Systems ideas have been around for centuries, but their application to human behavior is new. There will be a lag time in their acceptance as well. But the human does have the ability to think for himself and to get beyond the reactivity of parents, teachers, and psychotherapists. Professional people can control their own reactivity and calmly present all known sides of an issue. The more this can be achieved, the shorter will be the lag time for the acceptance of this new view of man.

Bowen's presentation next traced the development of psychotherapy from its roots which could be considered to extend back to prehuman evolution when mothers protected their young and individuals became aware of the importance of others. The instinctual forces creating enduring relationships are evident in many species. The early instinctual behavior continued as the primitive human forebrain developed.

As culture developed, clan members emerged to whom other members could turn for knowledge, guidance, and support. The human no doubt sought counsel from others besides his parents for certain crises that developed in his own life. As time passed, such roles became more specialized and professionalized. There were the early physicians, ministers, teachers, and experts in human relationships to whom people could turn for advice and guidance. This was true long before psychotherapy was identified as a profession.

Psychotherapy attained a new level with the work of Freud. Through most of the nineteenth century, treatment for mental problems was largely based on the assumption that structural defects existed in the patient's brain. Freud developed a completely different theory and a method of "talking therapy" that gave birth to psychoanalysis and, ultimately, revolutionized psychiatry and psychotherapy. The theory conceived of an unconscious which involved unacceptable sexual and social thoughts and impulses. Its intensity determined unexplained life outcomes. Through a process of free association in the presence of a nonjudgmental analyst, the patient could be treated.

Freud did the first detailed study of two-person relationship patterns. The patient replicated his early life attachments to parents with the analyst, a process called transference. The analyst had to master his countertransference lest he block the progress of the patient. If the analyst was unsuccessful, the patient was prone to act out the problem rather than learn about it. Freud required new analysts to have their own personal analysis in an effort to prevent this. While this procedure still holds in psychoanalytic training centers, the importance of countertransference has been lost in the recent surge in the number of people doing psychotherapy. Many new therapists believe transference and countertransference can be handled with a technical maneuver.

Freud developed psychoanalytic theory as an extension of medicine, and it was highly influential. Important changes occurred, however, during the first half of the twentieth century. Psychoanalysis was effective with the neuroses but not with more severe forms of illness. Therapy with severe problems required more activity from the analyst which necessarily involved more countertransference. The increased activity of the therapist resulted in the modification of psychoanalytic technique to "psychoanalytically oriented psychotherapy." The best therapists, however, still knew and respected the countertransference phenomenon. Another change in approach involved the "team concept." Psychiatric hospitals and clinics began using psychologists, social workers, and others as part of diagnostic treatment teams. Other major changes included the introduction of the major tranquilizers in 1954, the beginning of family therapy in 1957, and the Mental Health Act of 1963. The significant impact of the tranquilizers is well known. They have done more than anything else to change the practice of psychiatry in this century.

Family therapy burst into the professional world when it was discussed at a national meeting in March 1957. The theoretical jump from an individual to a family orientation had been slow and difficult. The principles of individual psychotherapy had placed numerous constraints on the therapist's involvement with the relatives of the patient. Years of work on theory, emotional connectedness, and transference had all gone into the creation of the theoretical basis for family therapy, but the average mental health professional was unaware of this. They heard family therapy as a simple shift in technique that could be taught as such to almost anyone. The field proliferated with professional people from different backgrounds who, in the rush to do therapy, bypassed theory. Group therapists became involved by putting multiple family members in the same group. Most new people to the field had not mastered the countertransference phenomenon in their formal training. They quickly learned and taught new techniques of family therapy. The field splintered into schools. In recent years, there has been some peripheral interest in theory, but the average effort goes back to issues that had been important before the therapy explosion. "The rapid change in family therapy has been an interesting phenomenon," said Bowen.

Enacted in the early 1960s, the purpose of the Mental Health Act was to make mental health services available to the masses. This reflected more social acceptance of psychiatry—it was not just for "crazy" people—and a shift from a focus on mental illness to mental health. The Mental Health Act helped consolidate forces that had been in process for a decade or two. These forces and changes had occurred too fast to be integrated. The changes were forced together during the 1960s. The focus was on brief therapy or "crisis intervention." Centers had large staffs of people who had been given "brief training" to do "brief therapy." Few had any understanding of the forces that create mental illness, and that these forces are more powerful than any rules that can be taught about their prevention and cure. Few understood how mental problems can be created in children despite parents' efforts to raise them the "right" way. While the Mental Health Act created a positive public image for mental health and psychotherapy, the negative side was the gradual awareness of the inadequacies of brief training.

Rapid changes have occurred in psychiatry during the past sixty to seventy years and particularly in the past twenty years. Psychoanalytic theory spread fast and dominated psychiatry. While the number of analysts was low, they were highly influential. Many psychoanalytic institutes appeared that were separate from medical schools. World War II changed psychiatric practice, making it a popular specialty. Many department chairmen were psychiatrists who were also psychoanalysts. At this point, psychoanalysis was closest to medicine. Many psychoanalysts even had the idealistic view that theoretical ideas could be taught as a way of preventing mental illness.

During the 1960s it became clearer that Freud had ideas that did not fit with science. This had really been known for a long time. There had been rumblings in the 1950s, but criticism of psychoanalytic ideas as "non-science" became more open during the 1960s. Medicine was based on an understanding of the biological factors in physical illness. So there was a gap between medicine and psychiatry, a gap that was really always there, but became more acknowledged.

The rumblings about "non-science" disappeared and the gap closed, however, when departments began appointing drug oriented psychiatrists as chairmen. Psychiatric residents began to have less training in psychotherapy and more training in drugs. Family therapy and the other psychotherapies were viewed as nonmedical and largely separate from medicine despite the evidence that psychological factors were important in every illness and that neurotic and psychotic problems were qualitatively the same. Medicine played an important role in accentuating this compartmentalization in its desire to bring psychiatry more in harmony with its basic assumption about the supremacy of biological factors in illness. "Go biological or else," was medicine's message to psychiatry. If psychiatry is biological, then it must give up its association with psychotherapy and family therapy. Everyone played a role in this split occurring. In 1977 family therapy was called a separate discipline by a national organization of family therapists. It became an autonomous discipline divorced from medicine.

Psychotherapy will always be there. How mankind will divide the disciplines is anybody's guess. Little is required to be licensed to do psychotherapy now, but the field is lost in terms of theory. Psychiatry has thrown out the baby with the bathwater, but it did it to be closer to medicine. Dr. Bowen concluded by saying that medicine will gradually move toward systems.

AN OBSTACLE TO "HEARING" BOWEN THEORY

MICHAEL E. KERR, MD

My original intention in writing a piece for this issue of the *Family Center Report* was to reflect on the year since Murray Bowen's death. What has been the impact of his death on the Georgetown Family Center, on the vast network of people interested in Bowen theory, and on the overall family movement in mental health?

In reflecting on the question of the impact of Bowen's death, I decided I did not have any clear answers. Many people have wondered for years about this question, especially those who had had some direct contact with Bowen. When you dealt with Bowen in person, you quickly realized the powerful force he was in the lives of those around him. It was natural to speculate about what people would do after he died. The only thing I am really clear about is that Bowen theory, despite the numerous misunderstandings that exist, continues to be important to many people, and the number is growing. Many of these people believe Bowen did as much as he could with the ideas, but there is a very great deal more to be done. People in many parts of the country are doing various kinds of research based on the theory. Conferences and seminars related to the theory are being conducted in many places, nationally and internationally.

What does all this activity portend for the twenty-first century? I do not know, but as my own sureness about the theoretical concepts grows, my conviction about the theory's future grows with it. Bowen was sure of where he stood theoretically. More than anything else, I think that sureness set him apart from others.

Published in Volume 12, No. 4, Fall 1991.

He was sure because he did the work and the thinking to become sure.

I believe Bowen theory will gradually alter how psychiatry and all of medicine is practiced. The broader frame of reference will do it. Man tends to fight getting a broader frame of reference, but eventually facts force it on him. Once people have a broader frame of reference, they act on it. Decisions are just made differently. The theory's impact will even go beyond medicine and be seen to have relevance to all manner of social problems. Problems are often unsolvable only because of the way they are thought about. Natural systems thinking will change the way a lot of things are thought about. Once we understood the physical forces in the universe, we could travel to the moon and beyond. Once we understand the emotional forces that govern life on this planet, then what becomes possible?

In any event, having commented on my original intention for this piece, I will get down to what I have actually done with it. I am going to talk about something very specific, namely, a common obstacle to people being able to "hear" Bowen theory. This obstacle was flourishing long before Bowen's death and, although I do not perceive it to be any more formidable than it ever was, it still seems as strong as ever. It is old stuff, but it is also current stuff. It has been discussed many times before. One could ask, "Is it useful to keep bringing up these matters?" I think it is because we are all so incredibly embedded in the emotional forces described by the theory that it is difficult to keep the influence of these forces in focus. The pull to lose perspective on the process is ever present. Murray Bowen was embedded in these forces too, but somehow got sufficiently "outside" them to describe them fairly objectively.

A concept that deserves repeated focus because it is so commonly misheard is *differentiation of self*. Much of my thinking about why many people have a difficult time "hearing" this concept has been influenced by having conducted numerous conferences on Bowen theory around the country. Some people "hear" this concept almost immediately. It simply makes sense to them. This does not mean that they totally grasp the concept, but they are attracted to elements of it that somehow ring true. Other people reject the concept almost immediately. Such people assume they understand what it means. They are uneasy. Something seems very "wrong" with the idea. Furthermore, since the idea is off base, then the person presenting it must be off base too. He probably has emotional problems of his own.

Outright rejection of the concept of differentiation of self certainly could reflect problems in the way the concept is presented. The presenter may be unsure of himself and unclear about the ideas. His unsureness may be manifested in a zealous approach. He tries to influence others instead of just stating what he thinks. His unsureness could also be manifested in criticism of other viewpoints, which turns people off. On the other hand, outright rejection of the concept can also occur when a presenter is very clear and not particularly invested in converting anyone. Negative responses to presentations of the concept of differentiation are to be understood, not bemoaned or decried. Such reactions are predictable, not aberrant.

Showing videotapes of clinical sessions done by therapists who have had a fairly good understanding of Bowen theory can be a superb means of eliciting people's negative reactions to the concept of differentiation. Oral and written presentations about the theory rarely have as much impact. People may be very positive about a lecture, but quite negative about what they see on a videotape of a clinical session.

Since negative reactions to clinical sessions are to be expected from a percentage of every audience, one could ask if it is worthwhile to show the sessions. I think it is for two reasons. First of all, an entire audience is never negative. Many people gain from hearing others talk about their efforts to think theoretically about their own lives and to act on the basis of that theoretical thinking. Second of all, the people who are negative, those who find the sessions disquieting, are stimulated to say what they think is wrong with therapy based on Bowen theory. Their responses highlight how this important concept is misheard and, as a consequence of being misheard, is either dismissed or pummeled into some unrecognizable form.

Most negative audience reactions to reasonably well done clinical sessions stem, I believe, from the feeling orientation of the viewer. A feeling orientation is not "good" or "bad," but it does carry with it certain expectations about what should transpire in a clinical session. People who have such an orientation get very concerned that something essential to the therapeutic process is missing in a session guided by Bowen theory.

The argument of a feeling-focused therapist goes like this. A therapist has a responsibility to sense and to elicit the feelings of the person being interviewed. The purpose of this approach is to help the "patient" become both more aware of his feelings and more capable of expressing his feelings. The inability to be aware of and to express feelings is seen as a prime cause of emotional problems. A therapeutic relationship by definition involves a "genuine" expression of feelings in clinical interview. The expression of feeling should come not only from the "patient" but also, to some extent, from the therapist. Feeling-focused therapists generally view a therapist's failure to elicit feelings in sessions as evidence that the therapist's theory is flawed and, more importantly, that the therapist has not dealt adequately with his own emotional problems.

Therapists with a feeling orientation are, of course, not all the same. Some can be relentless in their diagnosis of others. They do the same thing to the "patient" the family did to the patient. They take the omniscient attitude that they *know* what the patient is or should be feeling and relate to the patient as if their viewpoint is factual. Such therapists are usually not malicious, just misguided. The more vulnerable patients give into the therapist's pressure and accept his diagnosis to avoid upsetting the therapist. The patient may actually come to feel what the therapist thinks he should feel. This preserves the patient's comfortable relationship with the therapist, but the patient gives up self in the process. This is "family projection process 101" and occurs between a presenter and an audience as well as between a therapist and a patient. Of course, the process can work both ways: a patient can do it to the therapist and a presenter can do it to the audience. Generally, however, a therapist (by virtue of his status) and an audience (by virtue of its size and its potential for group process) occupy the "high ground" in the interaction, so the patient and the presenter are the most vulnerable.

A feeling orientation to therapy also represents a serious viewpoint in the mental health field. People gain something important from being more aware of their feelings and from having more ability to express them. A skilled therapist can be enormously valuable to his patients in this regard. There is nothing "wrong" with the feeling viewpoint, but differences in emotional functioning exist among the people who practice based on this viewpoint. Some feeling-focused practitioners respect "ego boundaries" far better than others. They do not exert emotional pressure on their patients to conform to their notions of what is "good" for people. These therapists simply try to represent the value they see in their point of view. However, even the therapists who are most thoughtful in their feeling-based approach are often disturbed by what they see in a clinical session guided by Bowen theory.

There are probably several ways to understand why feeling-oriented therapists are disturbed by sessions based on Bowen theory. Probably the most obvious way to understand it relates to the notion of the "therapeutic relationship." Feeling-oriented therapists frequently say they do not see any "therapy" in clinical sessions guided by Bowen theory. Some will acknowledge that the people being interviewed seem to be accomplishing something, but it is not at all clear what the therapist has had to do with their progress. Others will diagnose the people being interviewed as "intellectualizers," as not making any progress at all. They are viewed as talking about feelings, but not as "really" feeling.

The idea that a person can be helped in "talking therapy" without having to form an intense, feeling-based attachment to a therapist strongly conflicts with what is generally held about a "therapeutic relationship." A therapeutic relationship implies that therapy occurs largely within the boundaries of that relationship, so it must be fairly intense to achieve a therapeutic outcome. The idea of a therapist functioning in a way that minimizes the degree to which a person becomes emotionally focused on the therapist, and that *intrapsychic change is achievable based on such a relationship*, is foreign to a conventionally trained psychotherapist. So conventionally trained therapists not only see something missing in sessions based on Bowen theory, but the missing component is deemed essential to the therapeutic process.

Conventionally trained therapists tend to interpret what they see in therapy based on Bowen theory as the therapist and family member being emotionally distant from each other. In the absence of an alternative to a feeling-based frame of reference for conducting therapy, this relationship between therapist and family member almost has to be regarded as being dictated by an emotional problem, particularly a problem in the therapist. Why else would people act this way? An alternative frame of reference, of course, is differentiation of self.

Differentiation of self implies an ability to be in emotional contact with others while remaining "outside" the system. Two people can talk about the emotional process that can occur between them while only minimally activating that process. This is still an almost incomprehensible idea to most therapists. The point is to activate it, so the argument goes, so it can be examined and resolved. Without understanding contact with detachment, people interpret differentiation as emotional distance.

In a clinical session based on Bowen theory, the therapist is attempting to maintain differentiation in relationship to the family member. The therapist's effort stimulates the family member to do the same thing in relationship to the therapist. At its best, such a relationship permits the free exchange of thoughts and feelings on both sides. Since it is assumed that it is more productive for the family member to keep his emotional investment in existing relationships rather than in the relationship with the therapist, the therapy sessions look very different than conventionally based ones. The content of sessions includes some discussion of theory and considerable discussion of the relationship systems the family member is trying to understand and to become more differentiated in. There is not a rule against examining the therapist-family member relationship, but the goal is not to activate the family member's unresolved emotional attachments to others in the therapy session itself. *Intrapsychic change can occur through progress on intense relationships outside the therapy relationship.* Bowen theory, with its conceptualization of multiperson systems, makes it possible to work on self in the complex emotional arena of the real world.

Another way to understand the negative reactions to watching therapy based on Bowen theory may relate to a much broader issue, namely, the theory's conceptualization of the *emotional system*. The concept of the emotional system makes a distinction between emotion and feelings. Emotional process is considered synonymous with instinctual process, while feelings reflect the more superficial aspects of emotional functioning. This means that the feeling process is linked to the more basic emotional process.

The way people manage feelings is a reflection of forces operating in the emotionally governed relationship system. People are programmed to manage feelings in certain ways based on these forces. So while the awareness of and the ability to express feelings is important, its value is limited. There is much more to be seen and understood that governs human emotional functioning. So when the exchange between therapist and family member in a clinical session is influenced by the assumption that man, like other forms of life, is governed by an emotional system, an observer who does not hold that assumption will have great difficulty translating what he is seeing and hearing into something that makes sense to him. A collision of ways of thinking can trigger negative responses.

It took many centuries, but mankind, using its collective intellectual system, eventually defined fundamental forces and patterns in the solar system. The mass of humanity, heavily influenced by one another, held onto imagined notions about the planets long, long after the facts were known. The togetherness process retards the progression of ideas. In spite of countervailing winds, pioneering individuals have and will continue boldly to plunge forward, unearthing new facts and thinking differently about old facts. Bowen, using his intellectual system, defined fundamental forces and patterns in living relationship systems. Mankind's collective intellectual system will eventually define these forces and patterns in intricate detail. The mass of humanity, again heavily influenced by one another, will likely hold onto imagined notions about human behavior long after these facts are known. The togetherness process is not "bad;" it serves important functions in sustaining life. It does have certain consequences, however. Perhaps people will "hear" more quickly in the twenty-first century than they have in the past. I am not sure about that. For now, the task is to understand how this process plays out and to avoid getting caught in the polarization that inevitably occurs about it.

Responsibility for Self

Daniel V. Papero, PhD, MSSW

An increasingly common procedure in mental health practice today assigns several therapists to a family. A person may have an *individual therapist*, a married pair may have a *couples therapist*, a child may have a *child therapist*. Additional specialty therapists such as a biofeedback therapist, a hypnotherapist, or a psychiatrist may also be involved. A somewhat different version of the same phenomenon links several therapists to one person. In the arena of clinical supervision, a clinician may also have several clinical supervisors. An employer may require a supervisor within an agency, the clinician may select an additional supervisor in a particular area of interest, and may also see a therapist about some personal dilemma.

The likelihood is high that each of these therapists or supervisors has a different way of thinking about the nature of human behavior, of human problems and of how best to approach them. Even with a common orientation, transferences may exist between family members and the various therapists (or between supervisor and supervisee), complicating each person's ability to be responsible for and to represent self. From the viewpoint of Bowen theory, all symptoms are a product of the family emotional unit, and to divide them into separate problems to be addressed by different practitioners confuses the situation and adds additional relationship variables and triangles which can be extremely complex.

The main thrust of the effort to learn and apply Bowen theory occurs outside the clinical hour in the important relation-

Published in Volume 13, No. 2, Spring and Summer 1992.

ships of the family, the work system, and the community. The learning occurs in each family member's efforts to become familiar with the emotional system of family, work, and community and to manage self differently within it. The effort to improve functional differentiation of self is continual. A person's or family's efforts may occur in spurts and may or may not involve a clinician.

Basic to the effort to learn and apply Bowen theory is the person's understanding of responsibility for self. On a simple level, responsibility for one's life involves thinking through situations, making decisions, and accepting the consequences of those decisions. The process is more complex than it appears at first glance. How much thought and how much feeling should influence the decision-making process? And how do thought and feeling influence the acceptance of the consequences of decisions? Where do facts fit into the process? And what about relationships to other people? If a person and family understand and accept the notion of responsibility for self, multiple consultants provide no particular problem. But this is tricky territory indeed.

The general rationale for involving multiple clinicians in a family symptom generally includes the following arguments: (1) The individual/family is exposed to several viewpoints and ways of thinking about a problem. It is good to be exposed to several opinions and viewpoints. (2) Specialists may be particularly good at treating one kind of difficulty but not at another, and the patient benefits from the particular expert knowledge even if it is limited. The same arguments generally apply to retaining several supervisors and have merit.

Although rarely noted, the procedure may bring certain advantages to the therapists involved as well: (3) Each therapist may feel less anxious and less burdened if other therapists are involved. The patient may, in fact, benefit if the therapist is more relaxed. (4) The process fits better with the current medical model where specialists are frequently brought in to consult to the patient about a variety of problems. A team approach is highly regarded. To present oneself as a specialist and team player can lead to additional business, adding both to experience and income. (5) Where multiple clinicians are involved, one has to accept responsibility only for one's own small piece of the dilemma and someone else carries the burden of overall responsibility. These are also serious considerations, not to be dismissed lightly.

Multiple therapists/supervisors also present a number of dilemmas to the people involved. They can affect the therapists, but ultimately the individual/family comes to bear the outcome. Each of the common dilemmas has both subtle and overt forms, and resolution tends to be difficult. Central to all is the importance the person assigns to each therapist and each therapist to the other therapists or supervisors. In essence, the investment of life energy in another, whether by patient or therapist, is a major variable. The investment of life energy in others and the anxiety and reactivity that accompany it trigger the triangling process so familiar to students of the human family.

When a person or a family does not have a working understanding of responsibility for self, the involvement of others can compound the original problem. When anxiety is high, the varying viewpoints can confuse the person or family, intensifying helpless postures and reliance on outsiders to solve the problem. An anxious consultant can transfer anxiety to the person or family, disrupting a basic plan of action or reinforcing existing uncertainty. The clinician can promise a family a result that he or she cannot deliver and the family can act as if such a promise had been given.

Multiple clinical or supervisory relationships can impede the functioning of anyone involved, either clinician or patient. Tracing the difficulty is arduous and filled with blind alleys. A few of the more obvious examples follow. Many far more subtle dilemmas are also possible, each of which tends to disrupt a person's effort toward better functioning.

Therapists, even with a similar theoretical orientation, can become sensitive and reactive to the involvement of one another. This reactivity can be communicated in innumerable ways to the family or person being seen. When, for example, spouses each have a therapist, they may already be sensitive to the other's intense involvement with a therapist. The reactivity of the second therapist fits in with this sensitivity, confirming the person's mindset about the other's involvement. Often this occurs without any overt comment from either therapist about the other person's therapeutic involvement. One therapist's judgmental, critical reaction to another fuels the side-taking in the family.

The actual clinical approaches can collide with one another, and the family can choose sides as to whose therapist is right. One therapist may be pushing one person toward resolving internal conflicts and directly expressing feelings. The other may be coaching toward managing reactivity and ultimately differentiating a self. The more one expresses feelings, the more the other can become distant in imitation of self-management. The more the latter becomes distant, the more feelings are generated in the relationship for the other to express. Each can be encouraged by his or her therapist in this process, and the therapists can become sensitive and reactive to one another. The family can also maintain its relatively helpless attitude while the therapists work to solve the problem.

When transference has taken place, whether encouraged or not, the person's energy goes more into the therapy than into the family. The pouring of life energy into the therapeutic relationship can be as intense as an affair, and family members may react as if the patient were actually having an affair. This seems particularly common where a person sees a therapist for individual therapy, and the pair sees someone else for marital therapy. The one in individual therapy often sees the marital therapy as secondary and has little energy available for it. With more immature therapists, the individual therapist may advise the patient to do things that actually make the marital stalemate worse.

And finally, the therapists may actually take sides in the family dilemma, actively advocating for one against the other. This is akin to the alliance system of the great powers prior to the First World War. It provides at best an uneasy stalemate around the original problem and, in periods of heightened anxiety, can fuel a conflagration that might otherwise have been managed more thoughtfully and effectively.

In "From Couch to Coach," an unpublished abstract of a presentation given at the 1970 Annual Georgetown Family Symposium, Murray Bowen made the following observation about the efficacy of working out mature adult-to-adult relationships in one's own family. "From experience, any progress gained in the family of origin is automatically translated into the nuclear family." He speculated on why this "method is more effective than the others" [psychoanalysis and family psychotherapy for husband and wife]:

> The format of the method requires the trainee to accept responsibility for his own life, and to accept the working proposition that he, through his own effort, can modify his own family system. It is the only one of the three methods of psychoanalysis, family psychotherapy for the clinician and his or her spouse, and the coaching process with the extended family in which the trainee is completely on his own, without a therapist during significant emotional reactions, that occur during his visits with his family.[1]

---

[1] Murray Bowen. 1970. "From Couch to Coach," p. 1.

Although in this reference Bowen was talking about the training of family therapists, he highlights two important principles central to any effort to develop an application of Bowen theory: (1) the person accepts responsibility for his or her own life and (2) he or she accepts the working proposition that the family system can change in response to a change in self. As simple as these principles may sound, people do not seem to grasp them easily.

Bowen theory directs the person back to the original relationships or to their closest current approximation, downplaying the relationship to the coach. When the important relationships are activated, whether to a spouse, parent, or other significant emotional figure, and life energy is directed toward managing self in those relationships, the coach is effectively outside the transference, using knowledge of triangles to guide his or her behavior. The dilemma of transference can arise when seeing one person individually. To counter this possibility, Bowen refined the clinical skill which he called *staying outside the transference*.[2] He defined "staying out of the transference" as the clinician's ability to keep self emotionally disengaged. The clinician works to manage his or her sensitivity, interpretive mindset, and emotional reactivity to the other person.

The effort begins with initial contact with the family and the clinician's task of establishing the orientation of the theoretical-therapeutic system. Bowen describes his thinking in the following manner:

Most families are referred with a diagnosis for the dysfunction. They think in terms of the medical model and expect

---

[2] Murray Bowen. 1978. *Family Therapy in Clinical Practice.* New York: Jason Aronson.

that the therapist is going to change the diagnosed family member, or the parents may expect the therapist to show or tell them how to change the child without understanding and modifying their part in the family system. . . I persistently oppose the tendency of the family to view me as a "therapist.". . .When the therapist allows himself to become a "healer" or "repairman," the family goes into dysfunction to wait for the therapist to accomplish his work.[3]

Many of the familiar techniques associated with family systems therapy serve to accomplish this orienting task, including the basic idea of responsibility for self. This includes not diagnosing any family member, establishing the clinician as a consultant for the initial sessions and as supervisor of the effort if the process continues, and focusing on observation and research rather than therapy. The family makes a research project of itself.

Another aspect concerns the clinician's defining him- or herself to the family. Bowen explains what he means in the following excerpt.

One of the most important processes in this method of psychotherapy is the therapist's continuing attention to defining his "self" to the families. This begins from the first contact which defines this theoretical and therapeutic system and its differences from others. It proceeds in almost every session around all kinds of life issues. Of importance are the "action" stands which have to do with "what I will do and will not do." I believe a therapist is in poor position to ask a family to do something he does not do.[4]

---

[3] Bowen, pp. 157-158.

[4] Bowen, p. 177.

The positions defined by the clinician are always presented in terms of what he/she will or will not do, never in terms of what is best for the family.

Bowen sums up his basic notion of "staying out of the transference" in the following paragraph.

> The life style of this low level of differentiation is the invest-ment of psychic energy in the "self" of another. When this happens in therapy, it is transference. A goal of this therapy is to help the other person make a research project out of life. It is important to keep "self" contained with the therapist as [with] the other spouse. If the person understands the life-goal nature of the effort and that progress will slow down or stop with energy invested in the "self" of the therapist, he is in a better position to help keep the energy focused on the goal. [5]

To the degree that the clinician has been successful in func-tioning as a coach rather than therapist and in staying out of the transference, the dilemmas associated with the therapeutic rela-tionship can generally be avoided. Each clinician develops his or her way of presenting self and the theoretical-therapeutic ori-entation to the family. Some elements are relatively common, including the respectful attitude of the clinician toward the fam-ily, the relative infrequency of appointments, often determined by the family, and the focus on learning more about the family rather than fixing the family problem.

Common relationship dilemmas between clinician and fam-ily generally indicate that the clinician has not defined him- or herself clearly enough to the family. The family's behavior may

---

[5] Bowen, p. 179.

change agent, pressuring the family in the process to accept his or her interpretation of reality and to conduct themselves in the manner he or she deems appropriate. The clinician may not have defined his or her position adequately to the forces outside the clinical process itself and his or her behavior may represent that blurred boundary. The clinician may reflect the anxiety of the agency, the court system, and the broader society in his or her approach to the family, which responds with its own anxiety. What is called resistance can also reflect the beginning of a person's effort toward differentiation within the family. That effort may not match the clinician's notion of what ought to occur, creating anxious discomfort in the therapist who defines the patient as resistant. In short, the coach works always to see and modify his or her part of an emotional process.

From the first contact, therefore, the clinician works to define self to a clinical family. The family is responsible for its own decisions, and the coach for his or hers. Each can end participation in the clinical process at any time for any reason. This is not a matter of technique but built into the relationship between coach and family from the beginning. The ending of clinical contact can occur in innumerable ways. Typically the family decides when to begin and to end the contact. There is no concept of right timing, at least from the clinician. The family determines its priorities in much the same way it determines how often to see a personal physician, a banker, or any other sort of consultant. And the clinician determines how much he or she is willing to be seen. In short, the concept of termination applies to a different way to thinking about the relationship between clinician and family and a different focus and development of that relationship.

The involvement of several supervisors or consultants with the clinician incorporates all of the elements discussed above. The clinician can be expected to understand the impact of the triangling process and to conduct self with a respect for boundaries as an element of responsibility for self. When a person is aware of and has some ability to contain self within a relationship to a clinician or supervisor, and understands that he or she is alone to decide how to conduct oneself in life situations, and when one accepts responsibility for the consequences of his or her decisions and actions, a person can employ multiple consultants advantageously.

As a supervisor or clinician, one also has the responsibility to understand the dilemma presented by multiple therapists to a patient, family, or consulting clinician and to recognize the indicators of difficulty for the family. Each clinician/supervisor has to think through his or her own way of monitoring the situation and communicating his or her thinking to the family. The clinician demonstrates responsibility for self in how he or she conducts self in the clinical or supervisory relationship. A clinician is in a poor position to ask another to do something that the clinician does not understand and does not do him- or herself.

A Systems Model For Disease

Michael E. Kerr, MD

For many centuries medical diagnosis was restricted to a description of the patient's signs and symptoms. The discovery by Pasteur of the relationship of germs to disease dramatically changed medical diagnosis. It became possible to classify disease based on specific etiological agents, such as the tubercle bacillus as the cause of tuberculosis, for example. Most cancer research today continues in this mode of trying to identify specific viruses, genetic defects, or carcinogenic substances that might "cause" certain cancers. Such research is invaluable if specific agents or defects can be identified and treated so that a particular cancer may be rendered harmless. Identification of the pneumococcal bacterium and specific antibiotics to treat it, for example, has greatly lessened the danger of that type of pneumonia.

As time has passed, it has become evident that invasion by bacterium or virus does not necessarily lead to the development of a clinical disease. In fact, in the majority of instances people can live in perfect harmony with these invaders or even with the presence of genetic defects without developing a clinical syndrome. With this in mind, saying that the tubercle bacillus causes tuberculosis or that smoking causes cancer is not entirely accurate. In recent years, an attempt has been made to deal with this issue by proposing a theory of *multiple causes*.[1] This theory states that several conditions or factors must be present for a disease to develop. The presence of bacteria itself is not enough.

Published in Volume 2, No. 4, Fall 1980.

[1] 1965. *Health and the Community: Readings in the Philosophy and Science of Public Health*. Alfred H. Katz and Gene S. Felton, eds. New York: Free Press.

A systems model goes a step beyond the multiple cause model, conceptualizing the balance of the relationships between the various "causes" or factors as the critical determinant in the development of clinical disease. A systems model for understanding the mechanisms of disease attempts to define all the factors that interact to produce a particular clinical syndrome. Each factor has an impact on the others such that the behavior or activity of any one factor cannot be understood out of context from its relationship to the others. Clinical disease is not the result of the presence of any one or all of these factors but develops through a disturbance in the balance of the relationship system between them. This systems model does not preclude the possibility that a specific defect or agent may be found for a given disease, but the important question is what disturbs the harmonious balance of biological relationships that leads to clinical symptoms.

The author was taught the systems model of disease by one of his own diseases, *acne vulgaris*. Acne is a perifolliculitis, an inflammation surrounding the sebaceous follicles in the skin. Muir has defined the following mechanism in the development of an acne lesion.[2] *Corynebacterium acnes* is a bacterium that finds an occluded sebaceous follicle suitable for growth. This bacterium produces a potent lipase, an enzyme, that chemically reacts with sebum, the neutral fat substance normally produced by sebaceous glands, splitting the sebum into substances called free fatty acids. Unlike sebum, when these free fatty acids leak into the tissues surrounding the sebaceous glands they are potentially quite irritating to the tissues. The presence of the free fatty acids is usually associated with a significant inflammatory response, causing the area surrounding the sebaceous glands to become swollen and packed with white blood cells. It is this inflammatory reaction that produces the redness and swelling that

---

[2] 1976. *Muir's Textbook of Pathology.* J. R. Anderson, ed. Chapter 25. London: Edward Arnold Publishers.

gives the clinical picture of acne. It is the response of our own bodily armies, our own immunological system, that creates the picture of chaos and destruction we call disease. Since these are our own immunological armies, to what extent is their mobilization under our control? To what extent is the deployment of these armies in disease an unnecessary, even counterproductive overreaction to the situation?

There are many other interesting questions posed by the disease acne. For example, why do some people never get it? People with high sebum output and people with high concentrations of the corynebacterium on their skin have never experienced an acne reaction. Why do people have exacerbations and remissions of the disease?

Several years ago I began trying to identify some of the factors that influenced these cycles of activity in my own case. My exploration contributed significantly to the development of a systems model for disease.

The first factor I identified was the consumption of foods with high sugar content. I speculated, perhaps inaccurately, that the extra sugar energized the bacteria in some way, triggering more lipase production, free fatty acids and eventually an inflammatory response. Efforts to reduce sugar intake did lead to some improvement in the acne. The second factor I identified was mechanical irritation of the skin by shirt collars and shaving, for example. What was interesting, however, was the gradual realization that excessive sugar and mechanical irritation did not always trigger an acne response. At times these stimuli were tolerated or adapted to rather well.

The third factor identified proved to be the most difficult of all to really see. For some time my wife had been telling me that she thought that when I was under more stress the acne was more evident. It is one thing to be told that stress can be associated with acne, but it is another thing to really see a clear association between stress and the activity of a disease process within oneself. For me it took time and careful observation during repeated cycles of the disease to become convinced of a clear association between fluctuations in my level of chronic anxiety and fluctuations in the activity of the disease. But I did become convinced. When anxiety was low, significant sugar consumption and mechanical irritations could be tolerated with only mild skin reactions. When anxiety was high, severe exacerbations of acne could be avoided by carefully avoiding excess sugar and mechanical irritations. The combination of all three factors in high "dosage" produced the worst reactions. The interplay fascinated me.

Later on, I resorted to the use of low dosages of tetracycline on a regular basis to control the acne. College students flock to clinics around exam time for tetracycline to get through school pressures without having a full flowering of their acne. It usually works for them and did for me. Since no one is entirely certain about the exact mechanisms involved in acne, no one is sure why tetracycline can help control the disease. Originally, I had imagined it controlled the reproduction of bacteria. Later I heard that tetracycline interfered with the production of free fatty acids, thereby reducing the inflammatory reaction. In any event, it worked. But since I am one to take aspirin reluctantly, I never liked the idea of using tetracycline to control the acne. I did like the idea of no longer having to worry about eating foods with high sugar content.

The reliance on tetracycline continued for about two years. During that period, I learned a good deal about my anxiety and my ability to control it. Acne had been an important teacher about anxiety. Eventually it became possible to get along without the tetracycline, even while consuming foods high in sugar content and continuing to experience various mechanical irritations of the skin. The fact that I could control the activity of the disease process through the control of my anxiety was mind boggling.

To what extent is this possible with other diseases? This is not to say that the acne only disappears by reducing anxiety. Certainly other biological variables influence it. But when acne continues to be active, anxiety is unquestionably an important variable influencing the clinical course. Nor is this to say that people who have acne have it because of "psychological" problems. Anxiety is a universal phenomenon and acne is but one of a myriad of ways anxiety can be manifested.

It would be tempting to say that anxiety in acne is reflected in an overzealous inflammatory reaction. But it seems more accurate to think in terms of a systems model and say that anxiety disturbs the balance between all the various biological factors involved. What probably occurs is that as the process gains momentum, the activity of each factor (the bacteria, the enzymes, the white blood cells) is increasingly modified by the activity of every other factor through a series of feedback loops. The disturbance is in the total balance of the system rather than any one part being the culprit. In other words, the activity of the inflammatory cells may reflect what is going on with the bacteria, sebum, lipase, and free fatty acids but also, the activity of the bacteria, sebum, lipase, and free fatty acids may be a function of the overzealous inflammatory response. The important point is not to pick out any one factor and blame the process on it. All of the players are capable of living in harmony. The anxiety disrupts that harmony and turns peaceful coexistence into polarized confrontation. A quotation from Lewis Thomas offers a fitting conclusion for this idea:

> Our arsenals for fighting off bacteria are so powerful, and involve so many different defense mechanisms, that we are in more danger from them than from the invaders.[3]

---

[3] Lewis Thomas. 1974. *The Lives of a Cell*. New York: The Viking Press, Inc., p. 78.

The Importance of Beliefs, Emotions and Relationships in the Recovery from Cancer

Michael E. Kerr, MD

On April 11, 1981, The Georgetown Family Center sponsored its fourth symposium on cancer. The distinguished guest experts were Charles H. Goodrich, MD, Clinical Associate Professor of Medicine at Cornell Medical College and Harold Wise, MD, Associate Professor of Community Health at Albert Einstein College of Medicine and Director of The Family Center of Holistic Health at Montefiore Hospital in New York. Joining Doctors Wise and Goodrich on the program were Dr. Murray Bowen and Dr. Michael Kerr from Georgetown.

The conference was well attended and generated an atmosphere that is difficult to capture in writing. Wise and Goodrich brought two families from New York, both of whom had members who have experienced complete regressions of widespread cancers. The families presented their views on what had been important to them in the recovery process. In the afternoon, videotapes were shown of Albert Scheflen and Gregory Bateson, each discussing the thinking stimulated by their own experiences with cancer. Murray Bowen discussed both tapes.

Perhaps one of the strengths of the day was the avoidance of simplistic explanations about the interrelationship of emotional and biological variables in cancer. In fact, the day was more one of listening and observing than of imposing explanations. The nature of the presentations literally forced people's thinking into a broader perspective.

Published in Volume 3, No. 1, Fall 1981.

The evolution of thinking about some of the biological and emotional aspects of cancer will be presented first as a way of background to the content of this particular symposium. The trend in both areas has been to move from a focus on an individual cell or an individual person to a somewhat more systemic view.

Most people still have a difficult time conceiving of any connection between emotional factors and the development and course of cancer. Part of this difficulty may arise from the way many people think about cancer as a kind of irresistible force that pillages the body and is largely unresponsive to other influences. In fact, such a view, the old theory of cancer, was the basis for the radical surgical treatments of cancer. Cancer was initially thought to be a local disease that remained localized for a period of time and them spread in a predictable way, mostly through the lymph channels. The lymph nodes were viewed as a barrier to the spread. The old theory assumed that a cancer acted as an independent, autonomous entity, unaffected by the body's defense system, and that it did not spread by way of the blood.

In the mid 1950s, the bloodstream was revealed as an important route for spreading tumor cells from the primary site to distant organs. It was also learned that although lymph nodes may destroy tumor cells, they were not really a barrier to their spread. The idea that a tumor was an autonomous entity was also modified as their growth or dormancy was shown to be related to conditions in their environment, such as the body's defenses. So, rather than cancer being thought of as a local affliction that ultimately spread, a growing belief developed that it was a generalized, or systemic, disease probably from its inception. This change in thinking about cancer obviously has had great implications for therapy. We have moved from radical to more conservative surgical measures, such as from the radical mastectomy to even just the removal of the lump itself. Also more systemic therapies such as chemotherapy have been emphasized.

There are some other interesting facts about cancer. Cancer is often multifocal. Besides primary site, there is frequently microscopic evidence of tumor cells at other sites in the same tissue. This does not mean these other sites are the result of spread from the primary site but, rather, they are probably separate tumors arising at the same time. It is as if the whole tissue has become carrier-prone, rather than one cell running wild, multiplying and spreading. This, again, is a more systemic view of the problem. Interestingly, these microscopic cancers often do not progress to actual "disease." For example, twenty-five percent of breast cancer patients show evidence of cancer cells in the uninvolved breast, but far fewer develop a second tumor. Autopsy data of women over seventy who died of causes other than breast cancer showed that the percentage of those with microscopic breast cancer was nineteen times greater than the actual incidence of overt breast cancer in that age group. The point is that people are capable of living in harmony with cancer.

The overall incidence of cancer does not vary in different societies. This has led to cancer being called a phenomenon of the "human herd" with about twenty percent of humanity getting cancer regardless of the environment or health regimens. Lewis Thomas refers to this as "some sort of vulnerability to cancer in general that we do not understand." Cancer, then, is not very different from schizophrenia where the worldwide evidence is fairly consistent. It is as if the human herd consistently produces a certain amount of cancer and a certain amount of schizophrenia.

What all these facts about cancer suggest to me is that, ultimately, we must attempt to conceptualize cancer in terms of systems. Our thinking has been rooted in looking for the "cause" of cancer inside the cell. Obviously, there is much to be learned about cancer from looking inside cells, but thinking in terms of finding causes there narrowly limits the perspective. We must think toward *organizing principles* that cells are responsive to and regulated by. Thinking in terms of a faulty "defense system" is a somewhat broader view but still quite rudimentary and inadequate. We need a systems theory that can conceptualize the functioning of the human body.

In the same way that we are moving a little bit toward a systems way of thinking in reference to the biological aspects of cancer, some of the work in the field of cancer is also reflecting a slight shift towards a systems view of the emotional factors of cancer. Mostly, however, our work in the emotional factors of cancer has been based on theories rooted in the study of the individual, such as a psychoanalytic conceptualization of the cancer patient.

Yet the field has been and is loaded with innovative thinkers and courageous therapists. The word courageous may seem overstated, but there has been no great stampede to work in this area and those who have worked in it have been labeled, at times, "kooks indulging in unscientific mysticism." As far as I am concerned, there is a science to this field. It is just that there are so many not easily defined variables that the patterns are not clear. Man's thinking about the solar system was in a similarly confused state before Copernicus, Kepler, and Newton brought us to a systems framework there.

The literature about emotional factors in cancer is extensive, and there are certain standouts in the field. Lawrence LeShan, working from a psychoanalytic framework, has contributed extensively to the field. He emphasizes the significance of a loss of a relationship eight years to a few months prior to the diagnosis, a point emphasized by almost everyone who has worked in the field. He describes the person vulnerable to cancer as faced with insoluble life situations and an accompanying feeling of despair over the fact that they feel they have done nothing. He adds that these people are unable to express anger or resentment or to become aggressive in their defense. He describes them as nice, cooperative people who want to get along, but who tend to alienate themselves.

In my own work with cancer, I have found LeShan's observations quite consistent with my own. Dr. Caroline Thomas, the distinguished guest expert at our first symposium on cancer in 1977, has done extensive longitudinal studies of medical students at Johns Hopkins. The former medical students who later developed cancer reported different family attitudes in youth from those of their healthy classmates. They are described as "low gear people, little given to expressions of emotion, whose relationships with their parents had been cold and remote." [1] William Green and Arthur Schmale have both emphasized that disease occurs in a setting of emotional distress characterized by separation from a significant person or the loss of a major goal. The disease develops when a person feels alone, helpless, and hopeless. Claus Bahnson, whose approach is based on psychoanalytic theory, emphasizes the role of depression and many of the other previously mentioned factors. He also talks about a "complementarity" between somatic and emotional disorders such that irresolvable conflicts may build in a person to the extent that the only way out is psychosis, while in another person cancer may be the ultimate route. The Simontons echo the above mentioned work, emphasizing the loss of a serious love object occurring six to eighteen months prior to the diagnosis. "The loss has to be such, and the response to the loss such, that it engenders the feeling of helplessness and hopelessness." [2]

[1] Caroline B. Thomas and K. R. Duszynski. 1974. "Closeness to Parents and the Family Constellation in a Prospective Study of Five Disease States: Suicide, Mental Illness, Malignant Tumor, Hypertension, and Coronary Heart Disease." *Johns Hopkins Medical Journal* 134:251-270.

[2] O. Carl Simonton and Stephanie S. Simonton. 1975. "Belief Systems and Management of the Emotional Aspects of Malignancy." *Journal of Transpersonal Psychology* 7:29-47.

Stewart Wolf, the distinguished guest expert at the 1978 cancer symposium, has focused more on cardiovascular disease than cancer, but his work brings us forward to a new kind of conceptualization about the disease problem. While the previous people have talked about loss of relationships, their conceptualizations have basically pertained to the individual. Wolf's conceptualizations pertain to relationship networks. He has studied death rates from myocardial infarction in the town of Roseto, Pennsylvania. He has observed that the death rate from myocardial infarction in Roseto was only half that of surrounding towns. Only one person during a sixteen-year period died of a heart attack under the age of fifty-five. Their relatives who moved away approached the national norm for myocardial infarction. Wolf did extensive research into a variety of variables that might influence the differences, biological and otherwise. He concluded that a "natural cohesiveness" existed in Roseto. Family units were extremely close and naturally supportive, as was the community as a whole. There was essentially no poverty, no crime, and no coronaries. The elderly were respected and there was a low incidence of mental illness and senile dementia. Then as the social pattern of Roseto changed there was an upsurge in mortality from heart attacks, particularly among the "break away" families where myocardial infarction and sudden death began to occur in men in their forties.

Harold Wise and Charles Goodrich, this year's symposium experts, also look at relationship networks. Wise has made extensive studies of the healing process in tribal medicine, discovering that the oldest healing form involves bringing the whole clan together and "working things through" for 24 to 72 hours. Wise and Goodrich presented the view that there is a "healing force" within the family. When people get emotionally isolated from their family network, they seem more vulnerable to getting sick. If they do get sick, reactivating that network around the patient has tremendous healing potential. Wise and Goodrich are innovators. They are comfortable with what they don't know and have the motivation and courage to try new things. For a small percentage of cancer families in their practice, they have helped arrange family network meetings, sometimes at the bedside. In a still smaller percentage of instances, complete reversal of the cancer process has occurred. Wise believes that some day there will be a way to explain this observable phenomenon in scientific terms. What is important to me about their work, along with that of Dr. Stewart Wolf, is that it broadens the field of observation from just the individual patient to the relationship network. This broader view invites new conceptualizations.

Murray Bowen presented the videotapes of Albert Scheflen and Gregory Bateson. These, again, are tapes that must be seen to be fully appreciated. Scheflen emphasized how much our current blindness in understanding cancer is tied to being embedded in a cause-and-effect paradigm dating back at least to Aristotle. While man has moved toward systems in the physical sciences, he remains quite enmeshed in cause-and-effect thinking in the biological sciences. Much of Scheflen's thinking in the area was stimulated by dealing with the medical profession during his own illness. Bateson also described a different way of thinking about cancer, talking about disturbances in the ecology of the body that permit cancers to grow. He too had fascinating reports about personal experiences dealing with the profession. The effectiveness of the presentation of the two tapes was enhanced by Murray Bowen's having just recently been out of the hospital after a whole set of experiences of his own in dealing with the medical system.

REFERENCES

Bahnson, Claus. 1980. "Stress and Cancer: The State of the Art." *Psychosomatics* 21:975-981.

Green, William H. 1966. "The Psychosocial Setting of the Development of Leukemia and Lymphoma." *Annals of the New York Academy of Sciences* 125:794-801.

LeShan, Lawrence. 1966. "An Emotional Life History Pattern Associated with Neoplastic Disease." *Annals of the New York Academy of Sciences* 125:780-793.

Schmale, Arthur H. and H. P. Iker. 1966. "The Affect of Hopelessness and the Development of Cancer." *Psychosomatic Medicine* 28:714-721.

Wolf, Stewart. 1976. "Protective Social Forces that Counterbalance Stress." *Journal of the South Carolina Medical Association* 72:57-59.

FAMILY DIAGNOSIS AS A PREREQUISITE FOR PSYCHOTHERAPEUTIC TREATMENT

WALTER TOMAN, PhD

The typical family in Western Europe has two to three children and lives either in a small town or in the country. Recently, the trend has been more toward having one child, particularly in the larger cities. The average age difference between parents is three years with the husband being the older of the two. The parents are approximately twenty-seven and twenty-four when they marry, and they remain childless for two years before beginning to have children who are born at intervals of three to four years. There is far more variation in American families.

In ninety percent of families with children, the parents are present at least until their children reach adolescence. In ten percent, children have suffered the loss of a parent from death, divorce, separation or even absence since birth. In five percent of these families, children have lost a parent before they are six years old. Fatherless families are about five times more frequent than motherless families. In the United States, there are more incomplete and disrupted families than in Western Europe, particularly in the larger cities.

Published in Volume 2, No. 3, Summer/Fall 1980.

It is our pleasure to have Professor Walter Toman as our guest columnist for this issue of the Family Center Report. *Dr. Toman was our guest at the symposium on Birth Order in Family Therapy, October 9–10, 1980. Dr. Toman, author of* Family Constellation, *is well recognized for his studies on birth order. His work is distinctive in its focus on at least three generations of the family. He has provided a comprehensive systems understanding of the impact of birth order on a person's life course which is consistent with the concept of sibling position later developed by Dr. Murray Bowen.*

Sizeable deviation from this average family structure is usually psychologically significant. Large age differences between the spouses often imbue the older of the two more clearly with the parent role. Exceptionally large age differences from the children can transform the parents into psychological grandparents. Very small age differences from the children can transform the parents into psychological siblings. Both situations tend to weaken the role of parents as educators. Large age differences in age among the children separate them psychologically into quasi-onlys. Losses of family members have more traumatic effects the earlier they occur in the life of the child. If these losses are not replaced soon and well, the resulting insecurity in the bereaved may have long-term consequences in social relationships and mate selection. Temporary losses may also have traumatic effects, but they are usually milder than permanent ones.

Even if all the characteristics of the family structure are in the average range, the composition of children and the resulting family life can still be manifold. In a family of two children there are four combinations of children if age and sex are considered: two boys, a boy and a girl, a girl and a boy, two girls. This yields eight major types of sibling position for the children: older brother of a brother, b(b), younger brother of a brother, (b)b, older brother of a sister, b(s), younger brother of a sister, (s)b, older sister of a sister, s(s), younger sister of a sister, (s)s, older sister of a brother, s(b), and younger sister of a brother, (b)s. These sibling positions are elementary social roles that predispose a person in certain ways for permanent social relationships outside the family. Oldest siblings tend to take charge and assume responsibility for others and to identify with tasks and authority figures. Youngest siblings are more likely to lean on others and follow them, also to compete with them and to oppose them. A sibling of the opposite sex makes it easier for a person to deal with persons of the opposite sex, a sibling of the same sex with persons of the same sex. Contact and interactions with the other sex is more difficult for them, both in love relationships and in marriage.

More complicated sibling positions or sibling roles such as the older brother of a brother and a sister, b(bs), or the middle sister of two brothers, (b)s(b) are composed of the major types of sibling positions. Single children have no sibling position. They are used to life with parents and parent-like persons, but not to life with peers.

Compatibility of spouses and the quality of their life together depends, among other things, upon the compatibility of their sibling roles. The older brother of a sister and the younger sister of a brother, b(s)/(b)s, or the younger brother of a sister and the older sister of a brother, (s)b/s(b), have perfectly compatible or complementary sibling roles. In both instances the spouses are used to life with a peer of the other sex. Moreover, they supplement each other in their age ranks. On the other hand, couples like the older brother of a brother and the older sister of a sister, b(b)/s(s), or the younger brother of a brother and the younger sister of a sister, (b)b/(s)s, have an age-rank conflict as well as a sex conflict in their sibling roles. In both instances they have not been used to life with a peer of the other sex. Moreover, their age ranks are identical. Other sibling role combinations of spouses fall between the extremes of perfect compatibility and total incompatibility. Partial complementarity prevails if both spouses have several sibling roles but at least one among them that is complementary to at least one of the spouse's, like b(bs)/(b)s(b).

For only children life with peers is comparatively difficult. Single children differ from other single children, however, depending on the sibling positions of their same-sex parents. Life with peers is particularly difficult, if the single child's same-sex parent has been a single child himself. Life with a spouse is especially difficult if the spouse is also an only child. Complementarity or non-complementarity of sibling roles is relevant among same-sex friendships also. An older brother of a brother and a younger brother of a brother, b(b)/(b)b, tend to get along better with each other as friends than do two older brothers, b(b)/b(b), two younger brothers, (b)b/(b)b, or the older brother of a sister with the younger brother of a sister, b(s)/(s)b. For persons coming from a monosexual sibling configuration, same-sex friendships are of greater psychological importance, comparatively speaking, than they are for persons with siblings of the opposite sex. This is even true when those persons are married.

Relationships between parents and their children rest either on identification or on interaction and complementarity. Children predominantly identify with the same-sex parent and interact and supplement one another with the parent of the opposite sex. A relationship of identification develops more easily, the greater the similarity of the sibling roles of the child and the same-sex parent. The interactive relationship tends to be more successful, the greater the complementarity of the sibling roles of the child and the other-sex parent. In monosexual child configurations, both relationships with parents, those of identification and interaction, are more difficult.

The life situation and the problems of a client or patient in psychotherapy are often unintelligible without considering the structure of the family of origin. In order to understand his life situation some essential characteristics must be known. Besides those of residence, neighborhood, school and work in the past as well as at present, the family of origin and the family he has founded himself are among those characteristics. Psychotherapeutic goals can hardly be articulated without acquaintance with the social contexts from which a person has evolved. In order to decide whether a given psychological disturbance is due to a weak psychological constitution or to environmental influences (traumata), a patient's environment must be analyzed. Constitutional causes can ordinarily be inferred only indirectly, that is, from the absence of recognizable traumata. Depending upon the constitutional or environmental causation of a psychological disturbance, supportive or classical psychotherapy, respectively, are indicated.

Evaluation of the results of psychotherapy is impossible without knowing the patient's antecedent environmental conditions. This is particularly true if the interest extends to how the patient is faring years after psychotherapy has been terminated. In retrospect, antecedent environmental conditions, especially family background, appear fixed for a given person, at least in their essential characteristics, but they vary immensely from person to person. Patients begin psychotherapy from very different starting points and have very different distances to go toward health. The importance of environmental conditions holds true regardless of whether evaluation covers the therapeutic process, the termination of therapy, or even how the patients' children are faring in their own attempts to form families.

FAMILY DIAGNOSIS

MICHAEL E. KERR, MD

"Family diagnosis" began getting attention at Georgetown around 1979 or 1980 when DSM-III was being developed. At that time there was discussion within the American Psychiatric Association and within the American Family Therapy Association about including at least a few family variables in DSM-III. The problem was that no one in the family field had yet developed a system of family diagnosis. Murray Bowen believed such a system could be developed at Georgetown and he organized a group to work on it.

Initially, Dr. Bowen wanted to publish a family diagnostic manual but that goal was never realized. Nobody seemed satisfied that the two years of work had produced a diagnostic system sufficiently refined to merit publication. Then in the spring of 1984, Susan Barrows of W. W. Norton contacted Dr. Kerr and expressed interest in publishing a book based on Bowen's family systems theory. After considering the proposal for several months, Dr. Kerr developed the idea of orienting a book around family evaluation and including the system of family diagnosis developed several years earlier. Since Murray Bowen had spearheaded for developing the system, Dr. Kerr suggested the book be coauthored. Dr. Bowen agreed.

Dr. Kerr began writing the book in early 1985 and completed it in September 1987. Throughout the two and a half years of writing there were frequent discussions between Drs. Kerr and

Published in Volume 8, No. 4, Fall 1987.

On October 15, 1987, Dr. Michael Kerr gave a presentation at the Third Thursday Professional Meeting entitled "Family Diagnosis."

Bowen about theoretical points. Dr. Kerr did the actual writing and Dr. Bowen did not review its content. Dr. Bowen did write an introductory chapter for the book.[1] The book's title is *Family Evaluation: An Approach Based on Bowen Theory*. It will be available in June 1988.

The book consists of an introduction and ten chapters. Nine of the ten chapters focus on theory and the tenth chapter presents a system for organizing and interpreting the data collected in the family evaluation interview. This system reflects the work done on family diagnosis by Bowen, Kerr and others in the early 1980s.

The "diagnosis" of a family consists of making assessments in ten areas: (1) symptomatic person, (2) sibling position, (3) nuclear family emotional process, (4) stressors, (5) emotional reactivity, (6) nuclear family adaptiveness, (7) extended family stability and intactness, (8) emotional cutoff, (9) therapeutic focus, and (10) prognosis.

SYMPTOMATIC PERSON

The symptomatic person is the primary focus of conventional medical and psychiatric diagnosis. Defining which family member is dysfunctional and the nature of the clinical dysfunction is also the first step in family diagnosis. The category of symptoms (physical, emotional, or social) is described; for example, heart disease, kidney stone, agoraphobia, acute psychotic reaction, compulsive gambling, or shoplifting. The severity of the symptom is described last. Severity refers to the degree to which a person's functioning is impaired and can be described on a scale such as "0 to 4" or "1 to 10" or "mild to severe." If the presenting problem is marital conflict, the severity of the conflict is assessed.

---

[1] In fact, Dr. Bowen wrote an epilogue rather than an introduction due to time constraints and the publisher's deadline. —RRS

SIBLING POSITION

Sibling position is the second component of family diagnosis. Walter Toman's research on sibling position was incorporated into family systems theory in the early 1960s. Toman's theoretical premise is that certain fixed personality characteristics are determined by the original family configuration in which a child grows up. An individual is born into a sibling position. By virtue of being born into a specific position, the individual takes on the functions associated with it. An individual's personality is shaped, to some extent, by being in a certain functioning position in his family. An oldest child, for example, functions in certain predictable ways in relationship to his parents and younger siblings. The nature of his functioning shapes the development of his personality, and his personality, as it develops, shapes the nature of his functioning. Toman's sibling profiles are facts about families that transcend culture.

The entire configuration of the nuclear family is important in family diagnosis and there are several ways to record the information about each family member's sibling position. The positions are evident on a family diagram because siblings, whenever possible, are listed from left to right in order of their births. Toman has a different system. An older brother of a brother is symbolized as a b(b), a younger brother of a brother as (b)b, and a younger brother of a sister as (s)b. A sibling group can be shown as (b)s(b)(s), which denotes a girl who is the second of four children. She has an older brother, a younger brother, and a younger sister.

NUCLEAR FAMILY EMOTIONAL PROCESS

Nuclear family emotional process is the third component of family diagnosis. This component defines the flow of emotional process or patterns of emotional functioning in a nuclear family. The context of the symptoms is broadened from the individual to the nuclear family relationship system. The principal patterns of emotional functioning in a nuclear family are diagnosed on the basis of a careful history. If the functioning of one spouse has been chronically impaired for years, if the functioning of the other spouse has been largely unimpaired, if the functioning of the children has been largely unimpaired, and if the marriage has been harmonious, there is evidence that the nuclear family's undifferentiation has been bound primarily in the impaired functioning of one spouse. Of course, more than one important anxiety binding mechanism may exist in a family.

The flow of emotional process in a nuclear family can be recorded in several ways. It can be written as "dysfunction in a spouse," for example. It can also be symbolized with a variety of simple diagrams. All diagrams and symbols of family emotional process are at risk for being simplistic or reductionistic. Diagrams are also at risk for conveying the image of a static situation rather than a dynamic process. In spite of their shortcomings, however, diagrams of family emotional process are a reminder that a symptom in an individual reflects, in part, an emotional process in a family. The distinction between viewing a symptom as reflecting a "disease" confined within the boundaries of a "patient" and viewing a symptom as reflecting an emotional process that transcends the boundaries of a "patient" and encompasses the family relationship system is the major distinction between conventional medical or psychiatric diagnosis and family diagnosis.

STRESSORS

Defining the events or stressors that have disturbed the emotional equilibrium of a family is the fourth component of family diagnosis. After defining the specific events, an assessment is made of the overall level of stress on a family. Stress refers to an event, not to a family's reaction to the event. The emotionally driven chain reactions that can be set in motion in a family relationship system in response to an event are often a much greater source of stress to a family than the event itself. This fourth component of family diagnosis, however, is confined to describing the events themselves.

Stressors include events in the nuclear and extended families such as marriages, pregnancies, births, marital separations and divorces, serious illnesses and injuries, children leaving home, retirements, major job changes, financial setbacks, geographical relocations, and deaths. The magnitude of the events, the number of events, and the timing between events are used to determine the level of stress a family is under. The level of stress can be described on a scale such as "0 to 4" or "1 to 10" or "mild to severe."

EMOTIONAL REACTIVITY

The fifth component of family diagnosis is assessment of the level of emotional reactivity in a nuclear family. Assessment of the level of chronic anxiety or emotional reactivity is based on the number of symptoms in the family, the degree of functional impairment associated with those symptoms, the amount of distance and/or conflict in relationships, and the amount of anxiety and reactivity family members appear to have. Since there is no "meter" to measure anxiety or reactivity, a clinician usually assesses a particular family on the basis of comparisons with many other families. The usual scales such as "1 to 10" can be used to "quantify" impressions about the level of anxiety or emotional reactivity in a clinical family.

NUCLEAR FAMILY ADAPTIVENESS

Assessment of the level of adaptiveness of a nuclear family is the sixth component of family diagnosis. Adaptiveness is assessed by comparing a family's level of emotional reactivity with the level of stress it is experiencing. A high level of emotional reactivity in response to a low level of stress is consistent with a low level of adaptiveness. A low level of emotional reactivity in response to a high level of stress is consistent with a high level of adaptiveness. So this sixth component of family diagnosis is based largely on a comparison of assessments made in the fourth and fifth components. Level of adaptiveness parallels level of differentiation.

The degree of adaptiveness of a nuclear family is evaluated most accurately by examining the entire history of a nuclear family and not just recent events and the family's reactions to them. There may be several periods in a family's history when a series of stressful events converged and/or when symptoms were prominent. Assessment of a family's functioning in response to highly stressful periods and/or evaluation of the level of stress on a family during unusually symptomatic periods provides an impression about the family's overall adaptiveness. An impression formed from the assessment of several periods in a family's history is more reliable than an impression formed from just the recent period.

Adaptiveness can be described on the usual scales such as "1 to 10." The more experience a clinician has in family evaluation, the better able he or she is to make distinctions between levels of family adaptiveness. It takes experience to learn always to consider the degree of stress, the level of emotional reactivity, and the ways in which anxiety is bound in a family system when assessing a family's level of adaptiveness. Failure to consider one of these three variables or processes can result in quite erroneous impressions about a family.

EXTENDED FAMILY STABILITY AND INTACTNESS

The seventh component of family diagnosis is assessment of the stability and intactness of each spouse's extended family system. Stability refers to the average level of functioning of the members of an extended system. These parameters tend to parallel, but are not equivalent to, basic level of differentiation.

The stability and intactness of each spouse's extended family is evaluated separately. A scale such as "1 to 5" can be used to "quantify" the assessment. A value of "5" would be assigned to an extended family system in which the average level of functioning of a person's grandparents, aunts, uncles, cousins, parents, and siblings was stable in most aspects. There may be some problems in the family, but they are not major ones. In addition, an extended system assigned a value of "5" would be one in which a reasonable number of family members are alive and available to the nuclear family being evaluated. A value of "1" would be assigned to an extended family that presents the opposite picture: unstable and fragmented.

At this point in the development of family diagnosis based on family systems theory, the principal value of assigning a number to represent the stability and intactness of an extended family may simply be that it directs the clinician's attention to the importance of the extended family system in the emotional life of the nuclear family. A nuclear family cannot be understood adequately as a closed system. It is part of a larger multigenerational emotional matrix, and failure to consider the nature of that matrix leaves the clinician with a narrow perspective on a family's problems.

EMOTIONAL CUTOFF

Emotional cutoff is the eighth component of family diagnosis. All people have some degree of unresolved emotional attachment to their parents and larger extended family systems. The lower the level of differentiation of self, the greater the degree of unresolved attachment. People manage the unresolved attachments through varying degrees of emotional cutoff. Cutoff is accomplished through physical distance and/or emotional distance. A person who distances physically from his family often justifies it on the basis of its being necessary to gain independence from parents. He usually denies his emotional dependence on others and is prone to change relationships when the emotional climate becomes difficult to manage. The person who stays physically close to family often feels too dependent on it to leave. He may, however, cut off intrapsychically to manage the intensity of the attachment.

Evaluation of the degree of emotional cutoff is often difficult because all members of a family living in close physical proximity do not have the same degree of emotional contact with the family, and all the members of a family who are physically distant do not have the same degree of emotional contact. So physical distance or proximity is not a reliable indicator of emotional cutoff. Cutoff is evaluated on information about the quality of emotional contact between people. Emotional cutoff is at a minimum when people consistently act toward one another on the basis of mutual respect and are able to listen to one another without emotional reactivity interfering with ability to "hear" each other's thoughts and feelings. In addition, emotional cutoff is at a minimum when people do not have to invoke triangles to keep their relationship comfortable. An assessment of the degree of emotional cutoff can be "quantified" for each spouse on a scale such as "0 to 5."

THERAPEUTIC FOCUS

The data gathered in the family evaluation interview and the assessments made in the first eight components of family diagnosis are the basis for this ninth component, therapeutic focus. Therapy based on family systems theory, no matter what the nature of the clinical problem, is always governed by two basic principles: (1) a reduction of anxiety will relieve symptoms and (2) an increase in basic level of differentiation will improve adaptiveness. The early period of most therapy is concerned with the reduction of anxiety. As anxiety is reduced and therapy proceeds, the basic therapeutic effort is to facilitate differentiation of self. Most families that undergo therapy will experience a reduction of anxiety and symptoms. A smaller percentage of families will make some change in basic level of differentiation. Therapeutic focus refers to the issues and relationships that the therapist thinks, based on his assessment, will be the most constructive focus for reducing anxiety in the system and increasing basic level of differentiation. This focus may change during the course of therapy.

PROGNOSIS

Prognosis is the tenth and last component of family diagnosis. In conventional medical and psychiatric diagnosis, prognosis is based largely on an assessment of the nature of the "disease" within the individual. Diagnoses such as pancreatic cancer, congestive heart failure, cirrhosis of the liver, bipolar affective disorder, schizophrenia, anxiety disorder, alcoholism, conduct disorder, and antisocial personality have associated prognoses. For the majority of diagnoses, however, prognosis is not very specific. Too much clinical variation exists to allow a clinician to be precise. A "typical" course of multiple sclerosis does not exist. Some people go much longer that others without serious impairments in functioning. Nor does a "typical" course of manic-depression, alcoholism, or agoraphobia exist.

Every clinical diagnosis has an underlying biological substrate. There is a biology to schizophrenia, agoraphobia, and alcoholism just as there is a biology to cancer, rheumatoid arthritis, and nephritis. These biological processes must be taken into consideration when formulating a prognosis. The biology of all cancers, for example, is not the same. There is also a psychology to schizophrenia, agoraphobia, and alcoholism and probably a psychology to cancer, rheumatoid arthritis, and nephritis. These psychological processes must be taken into consideration when formulating a prognosis. The psychological makeup of all people who have cancer, for example, is not the same. These biological and psychological processes pertain to the individual. Family systems theory adds relationship variables, variables linked to the underlying emotional system that are believed to influence the course of all clinical dysfunctions. These relationship variables must be taken into consideration when formulating a prognosis.

Even with a careful assessment of all ten areas of family diagnosis, a clinician will frequently be "surprised" by "unpredictable" occurrences or non-occurrences. Poorly differentiated people with highly aggressive cancers sometimes recover, people who have lived on the wards of state mental hospitals for many years sometimes resume a reasonably functional life, and people who seem like excellent candidates for therapy sometimes do not change. This is part of what makes medicine and psychiatry so interesting. We are still more ignorant than we are smart. But the variables added by family systems theory are an important contribution to explaining and predicting more of what we observe.

THE FAMILY AS A UNIT

DANIEL V. PAPERO, PhD, MSSW

The Earth's great oceans, atmosphere, and land have always formed an interactive whole. The planet is believed to be
about 4,000 million years old. When life emerged to become a
fourth major component is not certain, but modern research has
pushed the date backwards to a moment at least 3,000 million
years ago.

The biosphere, that flexible amalgam of all living things
and their environment, is flexible and fluid. Its components shift
and move, adapting, adjusting, and responding to one another.
The earth is never at rest, and the biosphere is never static. The
atmosphere moves and swirls. Its component gases shift and
blend in ever new and mostly consistent and stable ways. The
land and the waters display similar fluctuations, again mostly
within a stable and consistent range. Living things, too, are mostly
consistent and stable.

From this perspective Earth is a system. A shift in any
element produces a response in others. The shift-response cycle
can be minimal, affecting only a few things within a small area.
It can also be global, altering the nature of the biosphere itself.
As a result, the modern planet is different from the swirling amalgam of gas and molten metal which emerged from the formation
of the solar system four or five billion years ago. It is different,
too, from the planet which produced living things three to four
billion years ago.

Living things have always had the capacity to influence
their environment. The earliest atmosphere had little oxygen,

Published in three parts in Volume 8, No. 3 and 4, and Volume 9, No. 1,
Summer and Fall 1987 and Winter 1988.

which was toxic to the microbial life which occupied Earth's niches (Margulis and Sagan). These living forms, essentially cells without nuclei, developed mechanisms to harness light and elements in the air and water to produce nutrients for themselves. In the process, these prokaryotic cells, as modern scientists classify them, released waste products. Other microbes developed the ability to utilize these wastes. Clearly the interdependence of living things was established early in life's development.

Microbes remain today the most abundant of living things. They occur in all environments known on the Earth and are essential for the proper functioning of other living creatures. They live independently and in conjunction with other forms of life. Such cohabitation is sometimes peaceful and sometimes deadly. Between one and one half and two billion years ago life took a second turn. A new kind of creature emerged which was radically different from the microbe. This new creature was the nucleated cell, or eukaryote.

So great is the gulf between prokaryotic and eukaryotic cells that some have called it the most important evolutionary development of all time (Margulis and Sagan). No one knows for sure how this development came about. One line of thinking suggests that the nucleated cell was produced when predator and prey prokaryotic cells formed a cooperative relationship. Instead of destroying the prey, the predator became incorporated into it. The enemies merged and became interdependent. Each maintained some of its original capabilities and assumed a function necessary for the other. Such thought suggests that cooperation was at least as important as competition in the process of evolution. The nucleated cell is the basis of all more complex organisms. All living things other than the microbes are formed from arrangements of nucleated cells cooperating with one another.

The eukaryotic cell is a naturally occurring system. Like the biosphere of which it is a part, the cell is flexibly fluid. Its parts are functionally interdependent. Without each part of the cell fulfilling its function, the survival of the cell is jeopardized. A shift in the functioning of one part produces shifts in the functioning of other parts. Each element of the living cell has the capacity to influence the whole and to respond to the influence of elements outside itself.

The shifting fluidity of the cell's interior results in certain processes or behaviors which are recognizable when one focuses on the cell as a whole. For example, food is imported, and by-products exported from the cell. A freestanding cell may move, altering its shape and its position relative to other parts of its environment. Reproduction occurs, replacing one cell with two identical ones.

Although the cell is shifting in response to a myriad of internal and external cues, its components have a particular interactional configuration or condition at any given moment. This condition can be thought of as the functional state of the cell. The cell's capabilities for maintenance and for behavior are determined by its functional state. The notion of health is really one functional state. A healthy cell has certain capabilities and options for behavior open to it which differ from those of a less healthy cell. A healthy cell behaves differently from an unhealthy one. The functional state of a cell may remain relatively stable over time, it may change slowly, or it may be altered rapidly. The functional state of a cell can be affected by factors within the cell itself and by interaction with the environment. In fact it is difficult if not impossible to separate these processes.

Organisms are composed of innumerable nucleated cells which have become specialized over time to create organs and perform specific functions within the system of cells. Like the cell, the organism is fluid and shifting. The notion of the functional state is applicable to the organism as well as to the cell. Processes operate continually, and the state of the organism is subject to continual variation. The component systems of the organism are also functionally interdependent. Each must perform in a specified way to allow the organism to maintain its health. Any variation affects the functional state of the organism and the well-being of any component element.

Each cell and each organism operates in accordance with a built-in guidance mechanism. For example, in the developing embryo, all cells begin alike but ultimately differentiate to become highly specialized. An animal moving along a forest runway changes gait, profile, and even direction in accordance with the capabilities of its guidance system. A sunflower in a field orients its blossom regularly toward the sun. Clearly some sort of interplay between environment and the living unit triggers processes within the individual which lead to specific behaviors and choices. Out of the scope of all possible behaviors, only a few appear at any given time. Furthermore, not all living things are capable of the same behaviors. For example, plant behavior differs in significant ways from animal behavior. Among animals some are more flexible than others. They are able to survive and even thrive under a range of environmental conditions.

The guidance system of the cell is basically biochemical. Chemical reactions are facilitated within and between the cell and its environment. Such reactions may alter the functional state of the cell. Some reactions occur regularly and repeatedly, forming the normal condition of the cell. Others occur rarely, and represent basic shifts in the state or condition of the cell.

The interaction between cells is also based in the biochemistry of each cell but also involves the behavior of cells as entire units. How a cell behaves influences the cells with which it comes into contact. For example, the T-cells of the human immune system regularly patrol the body, alert to the presence of invading microbes. They identify cells as self or nonself basically by means of chemical processes. When a foreign presence is located, the

T-cell moves aggressively upon the invader. The behavior of the T-cell has major implications for the cell with which it is in contact. Such interaction, therefore, is guided both by the processes within each cell and by the nature of the behavioral interaction. When a cell can influence another in an unexpected or unusual manner, something new occurs. The nature of the interaction changes. Such is the case, for example, between the AIDS virus and the cells of the immune system.

Such interactions determine the functional state and capabilities of the organism. The biochemistry of each cell within an organ determines its behavior. The behavior of each cell within the organ cluster of cells affects every other. How the cells interact together forms the behavior of the organ. The behavior of the organ affects other organ groups. The total biochemistry and behavior of cells, organ systems, and other components creates the behavior of the organism as an entity. Consequently the functioning of each cell underlies the functioning of all bodily components. Each component affects every other.

While all members of a species can be presumed to function in accordance with the same general guidance system, each particular individual differs from every other. One explanation for such difference suggests that the basis of variance is genetic. Some individuals have genes which influence morphology and functioning in one direction, and some have genes which lead it in another. A second explanation invokes experience of the individual as the basis for the variation.

When one considers the basis for individual variation as dichotomous (genes vs. experience), one greatly oversimplifies an extremely complex arena. There seems no clear way to separate the two in the development and functioning of the individual. DNA clearly provides the blueprint for developing the materials and governing the construction of the organism. If such development could be likened to the construction of a prefabricated house, the genes would provide the foundation, the preformed sections of the house, and the general placement of the materials in relation to one another. They would also lay the basic electrical and plumbing systems of the structure. Experience—the retained effects of the interaction of the developing organism with its environment—also plays a part. In terms of the construction analogy, experience could be compared to the various craftsmen whose work renders a basic structure operational. The master electrician, trim carpenter, plumber and so on all leave their mark on the finished house.

The evolutionary pathway leading to *Homo sapiens* produced a brain, a spinal column, and related peripheral nerve systems. There is a tendency to think of the central and peripheral nervous systems as the guidance system for the human. In a limited sense this is the case. The great neuronal net serves as a central coordinating and processing unit. Here signals of varying intensity from all over the organism are collected and processed. Some signals, such as the spinal reflex, undergo little processing while others follow complicated routes where they are modified in innumerable ways before a signal returns to a remote region of the body.

These great nerve networks are themselves a system with interdependent functioning. The central nervous system (CNS) is always active and shifting. Biochemical balances ebb and flow as hormones, neurotransmitters, and other molecules are released, taken up and held, or destroyed. Electrical activity shifts as nerve "circuits" become active or dormant. If each biochemical could be imagined to have a brilliant color, and the electrical activity of the CNS could be likened to a network of lights, then the CNS would seem a work of abstract modern art with fascinating blends of ever changing color and winking lights of varying intensity.

The CNS, with its central coordinating role, must clearly be considered an influential component in the guidance system of the individual. But each cell and each organ system also contribute. Like the medieval English monarchs who served *as primus inter pares*, the CNS may be first among equals. But its ascendancy is shaky, dependent upon the functioning of the other component elements of the organism.

Cells and organisms are fairly easily seen as units. They are, after all, self-contained within a boundary (the plasma membrane of the cell and the skin of the organism). Units larger than the individual organism, where such a clear delineation is lacking, are somewhat more difficult to comprehend. Nevertheless, such multi-individual units are the rule among the colonial invertebrates and the social insects (Wilson). Creatures like the Portuguese man-of-war, a colonial invertebrate well-known to ocean bathers of the eastern United States, are colonies of individual organisms which have evolved together to function as a unit. Such colonies frequently display functional interdependence. The social insects form colonies as well. Ants and termites live in large groups of individuals which appear to have the behavior of a unit. Individuals assume functional tasks for the colony (queen, soldier, worker), and the individual has little capacity to survive outside the colonial structure.

Such colonies appear to be guided by a system of interactions among the individuals which comprise the colony. Each individual plays a part. The idea of the functional state applies to the aggregate as well as the individual. For example, ant colonies rest, march, fight, and construct nests. Each activity could be seen as representing a functional state of the unit. That condition is shaped by the functioning of each individual and the clusters of individuals within the whole. Each organism contributes to the state of the unit and is influenced by that condition.

Such functioning can be observed among many mammalian species as well. The behavior of each animal plays a part in the functional state of the group, and the behavior of the group influences the well-being of each individual. Functioning as a unit is particularly evident in the defensive and hunting aggregates of many species.

Many mammals live in groups which are based loosely on kinship. At the core of such groupings is the reproductive female. The group may be comprised of several such females and their appendages (mates and offspring). Within the group various processes are evident which influence the overall condition of the assemblage and the behavior of each individual within it. For example, many primate groups display hierarchies. The males in the group occupy different social rankings determined to a large degree by the effect of individual differences on group interaction. Similar processes are evident among females as well and affect the well-being of each individual both immediately and over time.

The human family displays the characteristics of a living system. The unit is flexible and fluid. For the family, the question is not whether individuals respond to one another but how they respond. A shift in the functional state of the family is reflected in the state or condition of each individual organism. The shifts can be reflected behaviorally, or they may be contained within the body walls of the affected individuals. The implications of such a view are far-reaching. Not only can behavior be seen as a product of relationship, but the health of each family member may be directly related to the functional state of the family unit.

* * * * *

The basic structure of the human family is contained descriptively in the term nuclear family. The term has become so commonplace that one tends to lose sight of its fundamental accuracy. It stems from the observation that families appear to have an emotional center or nucleus to which family members and some other nonrelated individuals are responsively attached. From this viewpoint the family can be defined as the total number of individuals attached to an emotional nucleus.

The definition suggests a dual analogy. Atoms have nuclei around which attached particles whirl. Eukaryotic cells, from which all complex life forms are created, also have nuclei with which other components of the cell interact. Although there is a certain appeal in comparing the nuclear family to the atom or cell, each is an imperfect analogy. The family center seems to exert pressure on the individuals attached to it. The nature of the family can change as members are added or subtracted. The changes can be smooth or energetic. Although similar things can be said of the atom, the precise nature of the pressures or forces which hold the family together remains elusive. The clarity of measurable electromagnetic forces which apply to the atom cannot be replicated in the family. One can say only that family members act as if they are attached to one another.

The eukaryotic cell, unlike the atom, is a living unit. Its component elements are functionally interdependent and form a guidance system for the unit. The cell is a self-contained unit, and the family, at least overtly, is not. The analogy holds rather well, however, between the cell and the multicellular organism. The latter is essentially a composite of eukaryotic cells which are genetically identical but have differentiated to perform various functions necessary to the maintenance of the organism as a whole. The cells and the organ systems they form are functionally interdependent, and the organism is contained within a membranous barrier.

The term *emotion* or *emotional* as used in this definition of nuclear family requires further clarification. Darwin used the term to address underlying aspects of human and animal behavior which were broader than a single human culture and were evident across species. For example, certain facial configurations accompany internal states. Individuals from one culture easily recognize the look and identify the internal state simply on the basis of photographs of people from another quite different culture. Similarly, the manifestations of illness are universal. Such signs can be considered emotional. The external manifestations of emotion have a dual function. They signal an internal state and communicate it to other individuals.

In a broad sense, *emotion* can refer to all processes which guide the individual automatically within an environment. Emotion would include genetic factors, experientially acquired mechanisms, and the functional state of the unit at any moment. For example, all living things must somehow acquire nutrients. How they behave is, to a large extent, directed by the mandate to eat or be eaten. The functional state of the individual determines the immediate behavior, and the constant requirement to obtain food determines broad movements or patterns over time. For example, the organism's functional state influences when it feeds and rests. But patterns of migration and territorial range are also determined by such pressure. Such organization of immediate and long-term behavior can appropriately be called emotional.

The evolution of sexual reproduction opened another emotional arena. Males and females orient themselves toward one another, at least some of the time, and toward others of either sex who are seen as competitors. In addition, at least for some species, offspring spend a portion of their development literally attached to their mothers and an additional, longer period of time in a dependent status upon a caretaker, generally but not necessarily the mother.

Humans have apparently always formed units of parent and offspring. Other caretakers can be substituted, but the human organism seems to strive toward the parent-child unit whenever possible. It is, seemingly, a part of the human emotional system. The process begins with a breeding pair.

One is tempted to call the breeding pair the emotional nucleus of the family. This is the case for large numbers of people.

But many families are composed of a single parent and attached offspring. There are also examples of adoption, where families are formed around adults who act as caretakers for children to whom they have no genetic relationship. Such units appear to function as well as those formed from a breeding pair.

From this perspective, therefore, the primary caretaker of the young is seen as the emotional nucleus or center of the family. This role is inescapably filled by the mother during the child's intrauterine development. After birth, other possibilities exist. Generally speaking, however, the mother continues to serve this function across her lifetime. Said somewhat differently, the breeding female is the essential component of an emotional nucleus. After the birth of the infant, others may take over that function partially or totally, although usually the mother tends to maintain it herself.

The breeding male is clearly required for reproduction, but his role in the emotional nucleus of the family is much less fixed. While his presence may be limited only to copulation, there is clearly a tendency for the breeding male to become an element in the emotional nucleus. The interplay between the breeding pair greatly influences the functional state of the family as a unit.

The term *attachment* is frequently employed to refer to the relationship between male and female and between parent and child. While they are not overtly bound together, individuals act as if their behavior is linked to that of others. The breeding pair initially creates a habitat together. They also tend to divide tasks related to its maintenance and to their continued survival as a unit. In this sense, the male and female tend to become dependent upon one another. When one fails to function with regard to a common task, the other pays some price.

Were this interlocking of tasks the only mechanism of attachment between male and female, they could separate relatively easily by assuming responsibility for or by reclaiming for oneself tasks assumed by the other. Some disruption of functioning might occur for each, but generally the separation could be relatively easily accomplished. Variables which might affect the separation could include the length of time of the interdependency and the degree to which tasks had become separated into the exclusive domains of each. The experience of each in functioning independently prior to attachment would presumably also be of importance.

The linking of male and female in a breeding pair clearly has more to it than the simple exchange of tasks and responsibilities. The process leading to reproduction generally begins with a condition commonly known as "being in love." In this state each experiences feelings of personal well-being. At this point communication between male and female is open and relatively effortless. When "in love," people also display a narrowness of vision and a blindness to dilemmas which seem obvious to the non-involved observer.

The state or condition of "being in love" appears to involve processes within each individual on a very deep level. More than a psychological process, falling in love is an organismic experience. The changes in perception and behavior suggest clearly that biochemical changes are occurring and internal processes are altering themselves at least temporarily. The capacity to fall in love is within the emotional system of the organism.

Lehrman's study of ring doves (1964) provides one example of how an innate tendency might come to be played out in a particular environment. Although the processes of the ring dove and the human are not homologous, nevertheless, on the level of analogy, the birds are quite informative.

The reproductive cycle of behavior for the male and female ring dove involves specific changes in behavior over the course of the cycle. A complicated interplay between psychology and biology is involved. The entire cycle lasts about six weeks, moving through phases of courtship, selection of a nest site, nest building, copulation, egg-laying, incubation, and the production of crop-milk, a liquid secretion produced in the bird's crop on which the youngsters feed. After about six weeks, the cycle is complete, the young are launched, and the courting begins once again.

Each step in this process is accompanied by behavioral and physiological changes. For example, crop growth could be eliminated in males if the bird were removed from the nest before crop development began. If, however, the male were removed but placed in an adjacent cage separated from the nesting female by a transparent partition, crop growth would continue as if the male were actually participating in the incubation. Simply seeing the incubating female precipitates processes in the male leading to glandular activity altering the bird's physiology. In a similar vein, Lehrman was able to demonstrate that ovarian development in a similarly isolated female would occur, providing she could see a male performing in the manner of courtship.

Lehrman's results pointed to a subtle and complex relationship between external stimuli from the environment which lead to endocrinal changes within the individual and the effects of such hormonal activity on the behavior of the individual. Two sets of reciprocal interrelationships seem to be operative: (1) the effects of hormonal secretions on behavior and the effects of external stimuli, including the behavior of the animal itself, on hormonal secretion, and (2) the effects of the presence and behavior of one mate on the endocrine system of the other and vice-versa.

To the degree that such processes occur in the human, people become reciprocally responsive to one another acting in certain ways. The response is emotional in nature and affects the entire organism. Such interdependency can develop as a result of intense processes between individuals. The processes referred to as *parent-infant bonding* or *falling in love*, for example, lead to an interpersonal interlock, and the process known as grief may represent the adjustment of a person to the dissolution of such an interlock.

These processes would be marked by changes in the entire organism. They could be considered to be coded in the emotional system of the individual and expressed behaviorally when the functional state of the organism is appropriate. It may be that individuals are more or less receptive to such processes at certain developmental stages. They could take place at any time, but certain periods would be more favorable than others. In addition, other factors may contribute to the process. Frequent exposure to one another over time may be a factor. Repeated sexual activity, occupying the same space (particularly sleeping in the same bed or in close proximity), and joint exposure to anxiety-arousing situations in which one or both perceives the other as essential to personal well-being or even survival may play a role. The processes of pregnancy, birth, and parenting as they affect each individual are also influential.

Clearly human breeding pairs form an attachment or linkage of this general sort. It is a natural process. But not all mates link with one another to the same degree. Said somewhat differently, the functional state of each is influenced by the behavior of the other to a greater or lesser degree. Not all breeding pairs are alike in terms of the degree of linkage. The greater the degree of attachment, the greater the sensitivity of each to the other as manifested in the functional state of the individual and in the behavior of the breeding pair.

* * * * *

Shifts in the functional state of the individual can be noted in two general areas—in physical functioning and in mental activity. Shifts in physical functioning are often subtle and not easily noticed without instrumentation and training. The most obvious physical responses fall within the general area of anxiety and can be measured by biofeedback equipment. In response to the presence or absence of the partner (or even to thoughts about the partner) changes in heart rate, blood pressure, muscle tension, and other parameters can be observed. Presumably other changes may also occur within the organism which are not easily measured by non-invasive procedures.

Shifts in mental activity can also be noted both in the nature of the process itself and in the content of the individual's thinking. Shifts in the process of mental activity include the speed of mental activity, for example, either a slowing down or speeding up of mental processes, the breadth of perception, such as the ability to discriminate among stimuli or the exclusive focus on a limited number of stimuli, and in the feeling tone which accompanies the activity. Shifts can run the gamut from what would normally be considered psychotic to planned, responsible intellectual activity.

The behavior of the breeding pair also provides information as to the degree of attachment. In a general sense, attachment can be noted in the tolerance of each for difference and the measures which are brought into play when such tolerance is exceeded. In intensely linked pairs great efforts are made to minimize the appearance of difference. Male and female may dress alike, engage in the same activities, present the appearance of thinking alike about all subjects, and work to avoid all environmental and interpersonal interactions which might introduce difference. When differences arise (as they almost certainly will), the pair will go to great lengths to reestablish the sameness. Each may attempt to persuade or even force the other to give up the perceived difference. Or one may eliminate his or her own view or behavior to fit better with the change in the other. When the difference cannot be eliminated, severe conflict may erupt and the abrupt dissolution of the breeding unit may occur. The effort to maintain or re-establish the relationship can become so intense that decreases in functioning occur in other areas of life.

Less intensely attached pairs display greater tolerance for difference and direct more of their personal energy and resources to the attainment of other objectives outside the breeding unit.

The basic nuclear family structure is complete when a child is produced by the breeding pair. Arising from the linking of parental gametes, each infant begins life firmly attached to its mother. The developmental process of the infant can be described as one of increasing ability to function for oneself. The resolution of direct attachment to mother is achieved at birth. The resolution of emotional attachment is the task of subsequent years of development. How the parents or primary caretakers have progressed in their own developmental efforts is believed directly to affect the child's ability to attain functional independence.

While the basic structure of the person-to-be is incorporated in the genome, much finishing work remains. Experience—defined as the retained effects of the interaction of the developing organism with its environment—accounts for the further refinement of the individual. There can, of course, be differences in the basic genome which then influence the further development of the organism. Environmental factors may influence the impact of such differences, but the basic plan will unfold. Downs syndrome, for example, represents the unfolding of a genetic plan critically different from standard at a single chromosome.

The initial environment with which the embryo must contend is the uterus of its mother. This is primarily a chemical environment where subtle shifts in the balance of the mother's biochemistry are reflected in the fetus. The mother's ingestion of chemical substances can have severe consequences. Fetal alcohol syndrome is an example. The mother's nutritional state at certain fetal developmental points is also highly influential. Other aspects of the mother's functional state may have developmental consequences for the infant. For example, Suomi's studies of "laid back" and "uptight" rhesus macaque mothers and their infants suggest that the mother's functional state is highly significant for future functioning of the infant.

The functional state of the mother is the outcome of her responsiveness to her environment. An important element in the environment is her mate. Based on her degree of attachment to that male, the mother's functional state can shift frequently and/or dramatically in response to her perception of his behavior. Since he, in turn, also responds to her, the interplay between the breeding pair can influence the environment of the embryo and thus embryonic development.

The interplay between the functional states of the mother and of the infant has a nine-month history at the time of birth. The arrival of the infant leads to the process extending and possibly intensifying the linking of mother and child. The mother's role as caretaker is behaviorally more direct and not simply a matter of tending to her own health and well-being. Visual, olfactory, tactile, and auditory cues are experienced by each directly, and processes or patterns of responsiveness rapidly develop.

The extension of attachment between mother and infant is complete shortly after birth with the two fully sensitized and responsive to one another. A similar, parallel process occurs with the father or other primary caretaker shortly after the infant's birth. The speed, nature, and intensity of the infant's attachment to a nonmaternal caretaker is influenced by that individual's exposure to the infant and the mother's tolerance for the involvement of the other with her child.

Because of the intrauterine period of development, the process of birth, and the nursing role of the mother in early life, the infant is assumed initially to be more sensitive and responsive to the mother than to other caretakers. This implies that the infant has both a direct experience of another caretaker and a direct experience of the mother's reactivity to another caretaker. The infant has the direct perception of the other adult and a sensitivity to shifts in maternal functional state which occur in the presence of the other individual. In the basic unit of two parents and a child, therefore, three interlocking attachments are at work at any given moment—that of the breeding pair and of each parent with the child. Each relationship can influence every other one through the mechanism of shifts in functional state in each individual and the responsiveness of the others to those shifts.

This basic unit of the nuclear family is replicated as each additional child is added. The nuclear family can be described, therefore, as a series of interlocking triangles. Through such an interactional and responsive network of triangles, a shift in a particular individual or in a relationship can spread to affect the functional state and subsequently the behavior of others in the family. What affects any individual, therefore, can affect the whole, and what affects the whole can affect any individual.

The basic configuration of parents and child—a primary triangle—is alive with emotional activity. The functional state of each shifts constantly and behaviors change frequently. The developmental path of the unit is characterized by the developing ability of each person to be responsible for self. For the neonate such a progression is obvious. Gradually the youngster comes to feed himself, to crawl, to walk, to run without assistance, and to explore an ever widening environment. Mental development follows a similar progression marked by increasing awareness and the development of the ability to reason and to make increasingly complicated decisions.

What is less obvious is that the primary caretakers are involved in a similar process. From the initial state of being totally responsible for the infant's well-being and survival, each caretaker slowly moves toward the ability to contain the urge to do for the youngster and to allow him or her to assume more responsibility for self. This is a lengthy process spread across years. It requires that the caretaker be able to manage functional states in self which urge involvement with the child and to be able to allow the child a similar opportunity to learn to manage self. Where the caretaker is unable to accomplish this task, the development of the child is hindered or blocked. As a result, the child does not become as independent as he or she potentially could be, and remains attached to the primary triangle. Development is incomplete.

Such a limitation is of theoretical importance. To the degree that responsibility for self is not attained, a need for another is established. This need for another governs the degree to which the individual attaches to others throughout life. In addition, the inability of the caretakers and child to evolve toward independence establishes in the child a sensitivity to the functional state of each parent and a corresponding functional state in self which is the basis for a reactive behavior in the person and in the unit. This set of relationships to caretakers, established in the primary triangle, becomes a template for future relationships with a mate and offspring of equal intensity. Said somewhat differently, all future relationships become variations on a theme.

The emotional need for another can be described as partial separation of individuals or incomplete differentiation of self. The incomplete differentiation of caretakers and child is handled in a number of ways which ignore the basic developmental problem. The outcome is a series of maneuvers to manage the difficulty the attachment generates. The unit can remain in lifelong reactive contact, or the parties may break contact with one another and attempt to manage need for another elsewhere. No matter where the person turns, however, the need for another arises along with the sensitivity and reactivity which accompanies it.

What emerges from this view of family is a constellation of nuclear families across the generations linked by the incomplete differentiation of the people involved. Each breeding pair is linked to the nuclear families which produced the male and female. The person appears to remain sensitive and responsive to events which alter the functional state of the primary triangle and of the nuclear family in which one was born and raised. Such reactivity can produce disruption in the breeding pair and thus in the nuclear family of a succeeding generation. In addition, each partner's need for another, brought from the original nuclear family, places constraints upon the autonomy of each partner and upon the flexibility of the new unit. Limitations in flexibility and autonomy impinge upon parenting ability and the capacity of the unit to adapt effectively to changing conditions.

Each nuclear family, therefore, is the endpoint of countless nuclear families before it. It is also a way-station of human reproduction en route to other future generations of nuclear families. Each nuclear family is a unit, as is the broader, multigenerational constellation of nuclear families to which it belongs. The emotional need for another, established in each individual in each nuclear family but also the product of countless generations, links each generation to its past while at the same time it influences the future. Against this background of the family as a unit Bowen family systems theory takes shape.

REFERENCES

Margulis, Lynne and Dorion Sagan. 1986. *Micro Cosmos*. New York: Summit Books.

Wilson, Edward O. 1975. *Sociobiology: The New Synthesis*. Cambridge, Massachusetts: The Belknap Press of Harvard University.

Lehrman, David S. 1967 [1964]. "The Reproductive Behavior of Ring Doves." *Psychobiology*. James L. McGaugh, Norman M. Weinberger, and Richard E. Whelan, eds. San Francisco: W. H. Freeman and Company.

Suomi, Stephen. 1992. "Subjective Assessment of Reactivity Level and Personality Traits of Rhesus Monkeys." *International Journal of Primatology* 13:287-306.

CLINICAL ADDENDUM

MURRAY BOWEN, MD

Some clinical conference days provide feedback on things I had sort of forgotten. There was such a day in the spring of 1980 when some in the audience placed too much importance on the "kinesics" of body posture, mannerisms, facial expression, and other expressions of body language. I have been interested in this order of data for a long time. It is easily over-interpreted or misinterpreted. That is the subject of this clinical note.

Experience with these issues goes back to the early years of my NIMH research. Most of our theories about human relationships include the concepts of love, hate, devotion, anger, rage, and numerous other subjective states. It is next to impossible to prove scientifically the presence or absence of these feeling states, or measure them, without depending on what the human *says* about subjectivity. The difference between what the human *says* and what he *does* is notoriously discrepant.

Decades ago, psychology devised the "scientific" method. It was designed to find common denominators in this shifting sea of subjectivity, and ultimately to make the study of human relationships into a science acceptable to the accepted sciences. This has not occurred. I do not believe this can ever occur.

Early in the NIMH research I was looking for ways to define the *verifiable facts* of human relationships, and to bypass concepts based on subjectivity. The effort resulted in my beginning effort to view the human phenomenon the way Darwin had viewed the subhuman world. My critics of that period said it could not be done. They were right within their frame of reference. I was distantly right within my frame of reference. It is impossible for the human observer to get beyond his own bias

Published in Volume 2, No. 2, Spring 1980.

and subjectivity in viewing the emotional phenomenon of which he is a part.

I was asking only for an opportunity to go as far as I could in containing my subjectivity, in becoming the most objective observer that was humanly possible, and in avoiding the intermix of my uncontained subjectivity with that of the family. My effort contradicted one of the main premises of individual psychotherapy in which the therapist works for an effective emotional connectedness with the patient, which is known as transference, and which is viewed as the principal modality of change in psychotherapy.

The family seemed to be a favorable arena in which it would be possible to avoid a transference with any one person. The goal was to leave intense emotional relationships between the family members where they had developed and to remain outside the emotional conglomerate of the family. This has been the focus of my therapeutic effort over twenty-five years. I have written about it in detail. I have never achieved perfection, but it has been possible to attain a high level of therapeutic effectiveness and to teach this to highly motivated young therapists.

By the late 1950s I was talking about the advantages of "avoiding a transference." My critics were quick to say this was impossible, that the concept was inaccurate, and I should say I handled the transference well. The critics were right within their frame of reference and I was right within mine. It was an insoluble polarized debate in which the critics could not "hear" my viewpoint. I stopped the debate, but I did not stop the effort which led to the concepts of triangles and the differentiation of self. In recent years the more sophisticated systems concept of "emotional reactivity" has gone far in replacing the cumbersome polarized concepts of transference and counter-transference.

Part of my early effort was to focus on *action* which could be measured and validated and to defocus subjectivity which could not be verified. In 1956 a research associate, Robert H.

Dysinger, MD, did a paper, "The Action Dialogue in an Intense Relationship." It was a very simple premise in which words were tuned out and the relationship between a mother and daughter was evaluated in terms of gross action between them. The action told a more consistent story about the relationship than anything that was said. The paper was presented at the annual meeting of the American Psychiatric Association in May 1957. Neither the discussant nor the audience could really "hear" the concept, the professional response was negative, and the paper was never published. It did represent an early effort to get beyond subjectivity and into verifiable *facts* about relationships.

In the late 1950s, Scheflen and Birdwhistell began their research on body language at Eastern Pennsylvania Psychiatric Institute. Theirs was a sophisticated study in which they tuned out the sound and analyzed family relationships from microscopic action on sound movies. I was so fascinated by their effort that I stayed in personal contact with them and learned all I could as they developed the professional discipline of kinesics. The *action* between people tells its own story. From the standpoint of conventional theory, the action is out of conscious awareness and could be called the language of the unconscious. From a systems viewpoint I now think of it as automatic emotional reactivity. I worked hard to incorporate the knowledge of kinesics directly into family therapy. It was not as effective as I had hoped. By the early 1960s I abandoned it except as background knowledge for the therapist.

By the early 1960s kinesics was being taught in professional schools. At my various demonstrations of family therapy, there appeared an increasing number of young professional people who were zealous in their effort to read body language meaning into therapy sessions. At first I was pleased with the interest in this new body of knowledge. People tend to view any situation through what they have already learned, and the new knowledge seemed to provide a different dimension than the usual psychodynamic explanations. As a group, the kinesics people seemed more dogmatic. The attraction to kinesics may have been the promise of a new key to the language of the unconscious. However it came about, the kinesics people were persistent. It was not unusual for them to imply, "Through my knowledge, I know something about you that you don't know." Any attempt by me to explain a different way of viewing the clinical situation was often heard as my defensiveness and denial and further evidence of the accuracy of their observations.

Other experiences add another dimension to this note. In the 1950s mental health professionals began visiting the established family centers to learn about family therapy. My family programs have always attracted visitors and the number has increased each year. Average mental health professionals have fixed ideas about the nature of mental illness and psychotherapy and little ability to comprehend a theory different from the one they learned in training. They have no frame of reference to "hear" that the way a therapist *thinks* about a problem can be more important than what the therapist *does* in therapy. The visitors wanted to hear about family therapy and they viewed it as method, style, and technique appended to conventional theory. The average professional visitor would say, "I want to see you *work* with families so I can know exactly what you *do* in family therapy." In the beginning I would attempt to explain some of the basic differences, hoping it would enable them to get more from the visit. Very quickly I learned that the basic posture of a visitor was not likely to change and the explanations about differences could be counterproductive. I have kept explanations to a minimum except when the visitor's curiosity is aroused and they have a basis for hearing something different. Instead of offering explanations, I try to ask for the visitor's opinions about their perceptions. Over the years I have heard hundreds of misperceptions about the theory and the therapy. A visitor who is free to say what he thinks will often explain differences with interpretations of my psychopathology. And so goes the professional world. In recent years, however, there has been an increasing stream of visitors who have been attracted by the theory who are seriously interested in knowing more about it.

Another version of these experiences began in the mid-1960s as doctoral students began scientific studies of the different methods, styles, and techniques of well-known family therapists. The number of these increased rapidly until the early 1970s. Since then the doctoral studies have tended to focus on proving some aspect of the theory. The average early doctoral student would ask for audiotapes or videotapes of actual family therapy sessions. Most did not want to know what the therapist "thought" he was *doing* in therapy. If they did want the therapist's opinion, it was to contrast it with what the therapist actually *did*, as revealed by their scientific studies. Most of the students had well designed research plans for the numerous variables in the therapeutic relationship, but none had considered variables that would detect differences in theory. I cooperated with a number of these studies, hoping the researcher would stumble onto differences that would not fit into their research design. This did not happen. The research had been designed primarily for what the therapist and the family did in relation to each other. I knew most of the therapists with whom I was compared. Differences were explained in terms of the personal characteristics of the therapist. I was amazed at some of the accurate detail the studies revealed and equally amazed at important factors not even considered in the research design.

Ascribing meaning to body language came into full focus when the television camera was introduced into family therapy. I began regular videotaped family interviews to large professional audiences at the Medical College of Virginia in 1965. Two factors seemed important in this new focus on body language. One was the video cameramen who were "on their own" in focusing on what seemed important. A one-hour session with people sitting calmly can be rather dull. It was automatic for the camera people to do close up shots of anxious motion, mannerisms, and all kinds of body language. Camera crews were rotated frequently and it was difficult to dissuade them from this preoccupation with physical motion. The other factor was the tendency of the audience to focus on kinesics. I tried repeatedly to tell the audience that body language was important, but to focus too much on it would miss other things. The composition of the audience also kept changing, and each new group of students had visual evidence to support their knowledge about kinesics.

The video program began at a time when I was still teaching the "reversal" as therapeutic technique. The phenomenon that I have called reversal has been further developed by Haley and later by Selvini Palazzoli as the "therapeutic paradox." In the early 1970s I gave up the teaching of reversals as technique because poorly differentiated therapists were inept in the use of the reversal, and better defined therapists automatically used it successfully.

The "reversal" has a long history at Georgetown. It was developed in the early 1960s as part of the theoretical concept, *triangles*. Until that time my activity in psychotherapy had been rather formal, serious, and restrained. Then came the precise knowledge about triangles. When a family member, or the therapist, could "see" the step-by-step development of the triangle emotional complex, and that person could assume an opposite or different emotional posture than that dictated by the family emotional system, the emotional complex would immediately resolve or be "detriangled." This knowledge of triangles was used in two ways. First, it was taught to individual family members as a way for the individual to quickly resolve the immediate family problem. It was magical when it worked. This was developed into a precise therapeutic method that I used extensively in the early to mid 1960s. I abandoned the method because the motivated family members seemed to be acting more on information from outside self than from inside self, the change tended to be transient, and the family never seemed to know what to do when symptoms returned. The method was amazingly successful for short-term therapy. I believe that variations of this method have been incorporated into behavior modification therapy and parent effectiveness training.

The knowledge of triangles was also used by the therapist in avoiding emotional incorporation in the family system, or in "detriangling" self when he became emotionally involved. The term "reversal" came from the effort to find an opposite or different posture from that dictated by the family system. The reversal was an effective way for the therapist to defuse the intensity of emotionality in the family and stay in contact with the family while staying outside the emotionality. When a family is emotionally involved in an issue, the climate becomes overly serious. The reversal involves an ability to see the other side of the issue, to interject a bit of humor, to change the pace, and to remain casual in the face of family seriousness. There are literally dozens of techniques involved in this. The therapist who has done a reasonable job of differentiating a self in his family of origin can get the point, remain emotionally contained, and automatically devise his own techniques for effective reversals. The poorly differentiated therapist becomes emotionally involved in the family problem, is unable to contain his own emotionality, and has to rely on *techniques* to get himself out of the situation. His efforts at using reversals are heard as sarcastic, insensitive, and at the expense of the family. When this occurs, the family is probably right. This was the situation that led my Georgetown group to discontinue the teachings of reversals as therapeutic technique. By the early 1970s we had perfected the method of coaching trainees to differentiate a self in their own families.

The focus on kinesics and body language reached its peak in the video program at the Medical College of Virginia in the late 1960s. The camera operators never gave up their tendency to focus on kinesics in the families and also on any body language they could detect in me. This contributed to the tendency of the audience to read meaning into body language. There were always those who heard my explanations as denial and further evidence that their interpretations were right. Until that time my body action in family therapy was fairly calm and formal.

In the 1967–1968 period I consciously decided to stop talking about the subject and to do a body language reversal on the audience. My goal was to exaggerate my own body action to the point it would confuse the audience and make the observers unsure of their ready interpretations. No one noticed my first attempts. I kept on exaggerating to the point of ridiculousness with a variety of meaningless hand movements, scowls, smiles, slouching in the chair, leaning forward, leaning away, and other movements. As with verbal reversals, I tried to make the action reversals discontinuous with the emotional climate of the moment. The families in long-term therapy were the first to notice and laugh. Very quickly the camera operators stopped the focus on body motion and the audiences stopped reading meaning into body action except for an occasional very serious student of kinesics. As time passed, I discovered that body language reversals provided an additional dimension in maintaining emotional detachment from the seriousness in the family. I continue to use it periodically in intense situations. Newer generations of therapists tend to see this as a built-in characteristic in me rather than something purposely developed to deal with an emotional situation. The incident at the clinical conference in the spring of 1980 involved the discussion of a clinical session in which I was fairly quiet and a few people in the audience were determined to read meaning into body language. It reminded me of a dozen years ago.

Acute and Chronic Physical Dysfunction

Edward W. Beal, MD

At some point in their lives eight of every ten people on Earth will experience back pain. Lower back pain currently affects seventy-five million people in the United States alone and accounts for approximately ten percent of all visits to physicians. There are seven million new patients with low back pain each year.

Although it is difficult to substantiate, early man and his predecessors, while walking on all fours, had virtually no back pain. When man evolved from that four-legged individual to this more upstanding individual, he moved from a relatively permanently prone position to a more upright posture. Although walking in an upright position greatly enhanced man's mobility and range of functioning, this evolutionary advantage was solidified only at great expense in body adaptation: virtually 100 percent of the American population by age twenty has evidence of lumbar disc disease.

This paper will illustrate the advantages and disadvantages of this development and the necessary body adaptation. It will focus on the response patterns of bones, muscles and the individual person and their systematic interaction in the evolution of physical functioning and dysfunctioning known as low back pain.

The spinal column is a chain of blocks (the vertebrae), stacked one on the other and kept from collapsing by an exact system of muscles and ligaments that acts with synergistic and antagonistic precision. The lumbar vertebrae in particular are large and massive because of their weight-bearing function. The

Published in Volume 3, No. 2 Winter 1982.

task and function of the vertebrae, in conjunction with the pelvis, is to support the rest of the body. Individuals who cannot stand up for themselves in confrontation are frequently referred to as "spineless." This metaphysical concept obviously derives from the physical importance attached to the spine.

The vertebrae have two types of bony projections, one to which muscles attach and the other to which other bones attach, forming joint processes. The spinal cord floats through the center of the vertebrae, and the spinal nerves proceed through these tiny, bony notches, serving as the body's communications system, reporting pain from the periphery to the brain and sending messages from the brain instructing muscles to function in certain ways.

Between each vertebra lies the intervertebral space occupied by the intervertebral disc. A conceptually easy way to think about the spine is to look at the spine as a stack of alternating hockey pucks and jelly donuts. The hockey pucks correspond to the vertebrae and the jelly donuts (slightly stale and tough) correspond to the intervertebral discs. The vertebrae are insulated from one another by the jelly-donut-like consistency of the discs. The soft discs also permit the flexibility of bending the spine in any direction.

Man's spinal column functions best when it stands erect like a telephone pole. Yet what keeps it from falling apart or coming down? Just as a telephone pole has guide wire to weather the winds of a storm, similarly the spinal column has muscles and ligaments which function to attach it to all that surrounds it. As the telephone pole and guide wires bend with the wind of a storm, so do the spinal column and muscles bend with the stress of their environment.

When man developed the ability to stand erect and thereby increased his potential for mobility, his ability to maintain balance became more problematic. Switching from four feet to two is like turning a soda-pop bottle upside down. A man standing erect has the same inadequate base of support as does the inverted soda-pop bottle. This difference is highlighted by the fact that it takes man between two and three years to be able to learn to walk satisfactorily while it takes most four-legged mammals only a few weeks.

However, maintaining one's balance while maintaining one's mobility is not the only problem. Evolutionary adaptation to the advantage of walking is incomplete. The table of the pelvic bones upon which the spinal column rests is carried neither level to the ground nor perpendicular to the spinal column, but rather is tilted forward at a forty-degree angle. Thus, to keep the appropriate spinal alignment and body weight evenly distributed, an individual should walk with his/her body tilted forward at a forty-degree angle. Yet, for a variety of reasons, parents encourage children to walk and sit upright. Adhering to parental commands to walk upright with shoulders back requires a child to force the lumbar spine to bend backwards. This spinal adaptation, enabling one to walk upright, changes the body's weight distribution and badly deforms the entire spinal structure. An exaggerated forward lean keeps the spine in perfect alignment as it was at birth, whereas the acquired, erect position severely displaces the lumbar column backwards, producing a pronounced hollow in the back referred to medically as lumbar lordosis, or, more commonly, as swayback.

While maintaining the acquired erect posture, the body's weight is redistributed to the back edges of the vertebrae, significantly decreasing the spinal column's stability. A common analogy would be changing a stack of children's blocks from one that is evenly stacked to one in which the blocks were aligned less evenly along their edges. The second column of blocks is significantly less stable. Therefore this curve of the lumbar spinal column enabling man to walk upright requires a major shift of weight distribution to the back edge of the vertebrae and the discs. This added force and weight is transmitted to the soft discs, causing them eventually to bulge and/or rupture onto the spinal nerves passing alongside each disc. This compensatory mechanism of shifting the weight in order to walk upright is sufficiently prevalent that by twenty years of age 100 percent of the American population has a deformed lower lumbar disc.

This adaptive mechanism (shifting the weight on the structure of the spine) creates both acute and chronic problems. The chronic process, through the destruction of the disc, allows bone to grate on bone resulting in gradual dislocation of that joint which, in turn, puts constant pressure on the nerve. The chronic, constant pressure on the disc leads to periodic acute situations when the bony passage is so deduced that during any extreme backward bend of the spine the nerve is pinched, producing severe back and leg pain. The pinching of the nerve sends an immediate message to the brain in which the latter, without the intervention of consciousness, responds with a message to the muscles to pull tighter in order to enhance the stability of the lumbar vertebrae. Unfortunately pulling tighter is helpful in stabilizing the spinal column up to a point, after which it simply pinches the nerve more, possibly causing paralysis and requiring total bed rest.

The specific muscles involved in this process include the muscles of the back, buttocks, and abdomen as well as the short, strong muscles along the spinal processes of the spinal column. The back and abdominal muscles are the guide wires of the spinal column and exert their effect through interaction on the pelvic table. The back muscles lift the back of the pelvis and thereby increase the hollow in the back. They are opposed by the abdominal muscles which lift the front of the pelvis and decrease the hollow in the back. All things being equal, the strength of the back muscles should be equal to the strength of the abdominal muscles in order to keep the spinal column straight. However, the back muscles win hands down. Yet the side effect of becoming the strongest is that the back muscles become the shortest and the tightest and therefore increase the pressure on the back edges of the vertebrae and on the discs that separate them.

The function of muscles is the development of tension and shortening. Muscle contraction depends upon stimulation of the muscle by the nerve. Between contractions the muscles assume a relaxed state. The reactivity of the muscles to stimulation is an important characteristic—one over which the muscle itself exercises no control. If a muscle is stimulated once, there is a brief lag period between the arrival of the stimulus and the initiation of tension development. When the tension reaches a certain value, the muscle contracts. This contraction is transient and the muscle subsequently lengthens and returns to its relaxed condition. However, if the muscle is subject to repeated frequent stimuli, a condition over which the muscle has no control, the muscle will not relax between each stimulation but rather will remain in a contracted state referred to as tetany. The plateau of contraction is maintained until the muscle begins to fatigue, at which time it relaxes and goes into dysfunction. Constant stimulation results in a state of constant functioning or overfunctioning that eventually leads to temporary dysfunction.

Although the muscle can exercise no control over this process, the mind/body complex of each individual can. The basic reactivity to stimuli is a characteristic of all protoplasm. Although the muscle has no control over its own reactivity, the mind/body complex is built as a series of interlocking systems so that a later evolutionary structure such as the cerebral cortex can exert influence over an earlier-developing structure such as the muscle. The mind/body perceives the tension and/or pain produced by the bone-muscle-nerve relationship described above and is faced with three choices: (1) to continue functioning, (2) to reduce functioning, or (3) to modify reactivity to stress. All things being equal, there may be a balance among the three choices. To continue functioning requires living with or denying the pain or tension and carries the risk of more serious dysfunction. The second choice, to reduce functioning or to underfunction has the advantage of reducing symptoms. It may be a rational choice or it may be secondary to the inability to deal with the pain or tension or the inability to modify the reactivity to the tension. This choice has the advantage of preventing further dysfunction but the disadvantage of losing current functioning. The third choice, to reduce reactivity to stimulation, thereby permitting balanced functioning over time, requires the mind/brain complex to influence the reactivity of individual muscle groups significantly. A major disadvantage is that training the mind/brain complex to reduce the reactivity of the body is hard work.

Bowen family systems theory states that the human condition can be described according to various levels of functioning. Individuals whose life course leads to higher functioning are described as better differentiated, and those whose life course leads to lower functioning are described as more poorly differentiated. An index of one's level of differentiation is the ability to balance intellectual systems and emotional systems. Another functioning index of differentiation is a measure of the ability to maintain one's own functioning while maintaining significant emotional contact with past generations in one's own extended family. The intellectual and emotional systems can be thought of as a complex unit of protoplasm. The task of the individual is to maintain some balanced, integrated functioning between the two. The stimulus for the development of functioning is significant emotional contact with others, beginning with one's mother and own family. This stimulus/response pattern for mature intellectual/emotional systems can be measured just as the stimulus/response pattern of the adult muscle functioning. Adult individuals who return for significant emotional contact with their extended families report a period of time with enhanced functioning followed by a period of time in which there may be an acute or chronic imbalance between intellectual and emotional functioning. The loss of functioning comes for some people with just one or two-hour exposure to extended family and for other individuals after a two or three-day exposure to extended family. Just as the constant stimulus to the muscle results in fatigue and underfunctioning, a constant exposure to the stimulus of the extended family almost always results in a loss of functioning unless interrupted by physical space or time. Constant exposure to stimulation of muscles may result in the loss of functioning unless interrupted by physical space or time. Constant exposure to stimulation of muscles may result in the loss of functioning of the physical self. For many, constant uninterrupted exposure of the intellectual/emotional system to contact with extended family results in a loss of functioning of emotional self.

Although the following is the subject of another paper, the manner in which individuals respond to physical stress and symptoms, whether by overfunctioning or underfunctioning, may well have a correlation with how individuals respond to emotional stress within their extended family system.

Normal stimuli provoke appropriate body/mind responses resulting in performance. Supra-normal stimuli may provoke compensatory mechanisms such as overfunctioning and underfunctioning of related parts in response to stress. This paper illustrates the similarities in response patterns and compensatory mechanisms used by bones, muscles, and the individual person in the management of stress and tension perceived as low back pain.

Primary Care Medicine and the Family

Michael E. Kerr, MD

History

Family systems theory is a new theory about human functioning and behavior. It was developed by psychiatrist Murray Bowen over about a twenty-year period between the middle 1940s and the middle 1960s. Extensions of family theory have been developed by Bowen and his associates since that time. It is a fluid theory, not a fixed body of knowledge. Changes will continue to be made in the theory as more is learned in family research and in various branches of the life sciences.

The roots of family systems theory are anchored in two general areas: (1) research that has been done in many branches of the life sciences, particularly in biology and evolution; and (2) research that has been done on the nature of emotional processes in the human family. Freud's psychoanalytic theory was an extremely important contribution to our understanding of human emotional functioning and behavior. Many *facts* about human behavior defined by Freud and his followers can be incorporated into family systems theory. Many psychoanalytic *concepts*, however, cannot be incorporated. This is because these concepts are rooted more in imagination than in science. (Bowen has argued that Freud understood the uncertain base of many of his concepts far better than his followers did.) While psychoanalytic theory was an important contribution to the eventual development of family systems theory, two important assumptions

Published in Volume 9, No. 2, Spring 1988.

This is an edited version of a presentation made at Medical Grand Rounds, Kettering Medical Center in Kettering, Ohio on December 4, 1987.

of family theory sharply distinguish it from psychoanalytic theory: (1) the human is a product of evolution and part of nature, and (2) the emotional functioning of individuals is interlinked.

The first assumption that the human is a product of evolution and a part of nature implies that not only has human physical structure and functioning been shaped by the evolutionary process but that important aspects of human behavior have also been shaped by the evolutionary process. Human culture, with its spawning of values, ideals, and traditions, is an important influence on human behavior, but it is not an adequate explanation of human behavior. We know that the human body operates according to certain principles or "natural laws" it has in common with subhuman species. The human cardiovascular system, for example, operates the same as the chimpanzee cardiovascular system. Family systems theory assumes that human emotional functioning and behavior also operate in accordance with principles or natural laws that operate in the subhuman species. These principles or "laws" must be included in any theory of human behavior. The discovery of laws about human physical functioning has made medicine into more of a science. The discovery of laws about human behavior can make psychiatry into more of a science.

The second assumption that the emotional functioning of individuals is interlinked implies that explanations of human behavior that are based on the study of individuals are limited in scope. Freud listened carefully to his patients' feelings and subjective impressions about their past experiences, and he watched carefully as his patients distorted their relationships with him on the basis of their feelings and subjectivity. Based, in part, on what he heard and what he saw, he constructed an elegant theory. It is a theory that attempts to explain human functioning and behavior from the vantage point of the individual. It is also a theory that includes much of Freud's own subjectivity in its conceptualizations.

Family systems theory, in contrast, was constructed from facts about the ways people interact. Feelings about a relationship are one thing; the facts of a relationship are something else. When people feel neglected, it does not mean they are neglected. Feelings can be placed in the context of facts. Family theory conceptualizes patterns of human interaction and the effects of those patterns on the emotional reactions, feelings, subjectivity, and behavior of individuals. The emotional functioning of one individual is closely linked to the emotional functioning of other individuals who are connected to him. A systems theory is able to encompass this relationship process.

THEORETICAL OVERVIEW

Family systems theory conceptualizes the functioning of all nuclear families on a continuum. At one end of the continuum, the interaction between family members is strongly governed by needs, fears, anxieties, and subjectivity. At this end of the spectrum, family members think, feel, and act as if they are all inside the same "emotional skin." They operate in reaction to one another; there is no individuality in that sense. Family members appear to be "stuck together." In nuclear families at the other end of the continuum, family members are fairly calm and their interactions are strongly influenced by thoughts and principles. Needs and fears do not override family members' abilities to respect one another and to act responsibly. Individuals can think, feel, and act for themselves. They do not appear as if they are under the same emotional skin or stuck together. Family members have autonomy or individuality in the sense that they do not act strongly in reaction to one another. Nuclear families exist at many points between these extremes. An average for society is a little off the midline toward the stuck together end of the spectrum. Emotions, feelings, and subjectivity, in other words, are highly influential forces on much of human functioning and behavior.

Family systems theory posits that this continuum of functioning among nuclear families is produced by a multigenerational process. Every multigenerational family, given sufficient generations, produces nuclear families at all points along this continuum. The theory posits that the changes that lead to differences in functioning among nuclear families occur gradually over the course of many generations. Furthermore, these changes do not occur randomly but are the product of an orderly and predictable process. The components of this multigenerational process include biological, psychological, and relationship variables that are so intertwined that, for the most part, they cannot be treated as if they operate independently of each other. The various outcomes of the multigenerational process, in other words, are determined by multiple factors that range all the way from genes to values.

Clinical symptoms of all types (physical illness, emotional illness, and social acting-out problems) occur much more frequently in nuclear families at the most stuck together end of the continuum than in nuclear families at the opposite end. In addition, the more stuck together the family, the greater the likelihood that symptoms will be severe and that they will occur in fairly young people. It is important to remember that a stuck together family is not equivalent to a "close" family. Emotional "stuck togetherness" can be manifested in people clinging to one another (clinging is not emotional closeness) or it can also be manifested in people being so reactive to one another that they enforce marked degrees of distance. The greater the degree of stuck togetherness, in other words, the more difficulty people have either not being very overinvolved or not being very underinvolved in one another's lives. The less stuck together people are, the greater their capacity for emotional closeness. Nuclear families at the least stuck together end of the continuum can develop symptoms, but the symptoms tend to be less severe and the recoveries tend to be complete. If the symptoms are severe, they are more likely to occur in fairly old family members, people who have already lived productive lives. Nuclear families at various points along the continuum reflect gradations of change in the frequency and severity of symptoms.

Research on the distribution of illness in population done more than thirty years ago by Hinkle and his colleagues is consistent with the symptom continuum described by family systems theory. Hinkle studied the incidence of illness in a variety of populations of unrelated people and found that the incidence of illness was not distributed uniformly throughout a given population. In a group of telephone company employees, for example, he found that ten percent of the group had a risk of being ill that was double that for the group at large. This ten percent experienced thirty-four percent of the total disability of the group. In contrast, the healthiest ten percent of the group contributed only one percent of the overall disability. This illness distribution was the same for both major and minor illnesses. In another sample of ninety-six American working women, Hinkle found that over a twenty-year period half of all episodes of illness occurred in just twenty-five percent of the women. These women had illnesses involving many organ systems. Another twenty-five percent of the same population accounted for fewer than ten percent of all illnesses, major and minor. The remaining half of the population showed gradations between these extremes. This general range of illness distribution held throughout, regardless of the population Hinkle studied.

An implication of Hinkle's research is that people differ in their susceptibility to develop clinical symptoms. The development of symptoms can be understood as related to the interplay of the following two primary variables: (1) degree of exposure to potentially *pathogenic* influences, such as genetic predispositions, bacteria, and environmental toxins, and (2) an organism's ability to *adapt* sufficiently to whatever pathogenic influences it encounters such that it does not develop clinical symptoms. That Hinkle's research was done on a variety of populations over extended periods of time and that his findings were generally consistent from study to study suggests that the disproportionate distribution of illnesses in the populations resulted from different degrees of individual adaptiveness rather than from different degrees of exposure to potentially pathogenic influences. This is the same basic idea posited by family systems theory: individuals (and nuclear family units) differ in their level of adaptiveness, a difference that is the outcome of a multigenerational process. The lower the degree of adaptiveness (or the more stuck together the family system), the higher the incidence of clinical symptoms of all types and the more likely it is that these symptoms will occur fairly early in life and be associated with marked functional impairment.

APPLICATION

It is not possible in a brief time to present enough about family theory to provide an adequate bridge for understanding its application to clinical situations. As a consequence, the brief clinical history that I will present next may not seem adequately connected to the theoretical ideas I have just presented. Regardless, however, of whether I have been able to demonstrate adequately a connection between theory and practice, theory and practice are most definitely connected. The clinical case is of a family with a ten-year-old son who has asthma. This nuclear family is in about the mid-range on the continuum of adaptiveness. Families at this level can develop symptoms during periods of moderate to high stress, but they function without symptoms during calmer periods. Such an adjustment can be contrasted with that of poorly adaptive families, which are almost never free of major symptoms.

The nuclear family, which lives in Washington, D.C., consists of the father, thirty-five years old; the mother, thirty-three years old, an older daughter, twelve years old; and a younger son, ten years old. The mother is the middle of three children from a family in Philadelphia. She has an older brother, thirty-six years old, and a younger sister, twenty-nine years old. Both of her siblings are married and live in the Philadelphia area. The brother has two children; the sister has none. The father is the oldest of four children from a family in Dover, Delaware. The father's mother died of a heart attack in 1975. His father remarried and still lives in Dover. A younger brother and two younger sisters are all married. All have children and all live in the Dover area.

The parents sought family therapy in December 1986 because the husband had announced that he was considering leaving the marriage. He had become romantically involved with another woman. There had been a significant amount of distance and conflict in the couple's fourteen-year marriage, so the revelation of his extramarital relationship was not a complete surprise to the wife. But there were two additional circumstances that were having a major impact on this family. One circumstance was that in May 1986, the husband accepted a new job that necessitated, at least during the first year of the job, considerable international travel. He was away much more than he was home. A second circumstance was that in June 1986, the wife's father, who still lived in Philadelphia, was diagnosed as having widely metastatic cancer. It seemed unlikely that he would live more than six months. So the family was reacting to two important events, and it was during this period that the ten-year-old son's asthma became much worse. In the fall of 1986, he was hospitalized twice with pneumonia. He also had many school absences due to asthmatic symptoms, even when he was not in the hospital. This boy's asthma had been diagnosed four years earlier, but he had not had significant symptoms until the fall of 1986.

The therapy, which included only the husband and wife, proved helpful in several areas: for the marriage, for the wife's efforts to manage herself in her extended family during the final months of her father's life, and for the wife's efforts to better understand her relationship with her son. The husband was able to see some of his part in helping to create the very characteristics in his wife that "caused" him to reject her. On the wife's side, she saw that when she got especially anxious, she focused intensely on what was "wrong" with her husband and on what he was "not doing" for her and the children. She could easily see that the negative focus drove him away from her. The wife also saw how overinvolved and frustrated she got with her son's physical problems. Her anxiety was often channeled into focusing on his health and well-being. She also gained a better appreciation of how reactive or "sensitized" her son was to her being upset. The boy was much more reactive than his older sister to family tension.

By the late spring of 1987, after about five months of therapy, the husband had ended his extramarital relationship and the marriage was much calmer. The two spouses were talking more and "hearing" each other better than they had in many years. The key to the rapid progress was the ease with which both spouses were able to forego their tendencies to blame each other for whatever problems existed. Both spouses made strong efforts to see themselves as part of the problem, as "part of the system." The wife's father died in early March. The wife's extended family stayed in excellent emotional contact with one another during the weeks prior to the father's death. The excellent level of contact and support among the family was partly due to the wife's efforts to manage herself effectively. A dying person can become isolated by the anxiety of those around him, and the family members can become reactively isolated from one another during the period in which someone is dying. This did not happen in this family. The father died peacefully and the wife, her mother, and her siblings have made a good adjustment since his death. This couple's ten-year-old son has been remarkably symptom-free throughout most of this year and has not missed any school this fall.

I do not think it was a coincidence that the son's asthma was much worse during the protracted period of high family anxiety. High family anxiety did not cause his symptoms, but it was, in my opinion, an important influence, perhaps the most important influence, on them. It is common for parents to be more involved emotionally with one child than with the others. It is important to recognize this overinvolvement because it is the most involved child who tends to be the most reactive to family anxiety. He or she is highly prone to express family anxiety in some type of symptoms. The symptoms may be in the form of physical illness, emotional illness, or social acting-out problems. It is also important to recognize that parents tend to be the most reactive to anxiety or problems in the child with whom they are most overinvolved. They do not ignore the other children, but they are usually a little calmer and more realistic in dealing with them.

An important contribution of a family viewpoint is the recognition that *a symptom transcends the boundary of the symptomatic individual.* An individual is not so autonomous that his symptoms can be understood in isolation from the prevailing "emotional winds" of his central relationship network. For most people, the family is the most important component of their relationship network, although nonfamilial relationships are also important to consider. From the standpoint of family systems theory, an evaluation of a clinical symptom necessitates evaluation of the nuclear and extended family systems. Important questions about the extended systems include: Who are the people? Where are the people? What is happening with them? Family members are, for obvious reasons, anxious about whatever symptoms that exist but, if a clinician has a broad focus, the family is often able to broaden its focus too. If people can think about what is happening instead of just reacting to it, possibilities for dealing with the situation differently usually come into view.

DOCTOR-PATIENT RELATIONSHIP

I am sure that I do not need to emphasize the importance of the doctor-patient relationship to anyone here. Few would argue the point, I believe, that the characteristics of a patient's relationship with his doctor—and the entire medical system—can frequently promote or undermine recovery. A lesson that has been learned in family psychiatry is that the model of a patient telling the doctor his symptoms, the doctor diagnosing the problem, and the doctor "fixing" the patient can often be a problem *for the patient*. This model usually works very well in the diagnosis and treatment of acute problems, but it does not work very well for chronic problems. When a patient takes a passive role, treating the doctor as the one who "knows," the doctor can get into a position of trying to provide answers he does not have. Some patients insist that the doctor is an "expert" who should tell them what to do. If the doctor fails to do this, they will get another doctor. Most patients, however, have more internal resources and can be more realistic about what their doctors can provide.

I suppose this point about active doctor/passive patient is both simple and obvious, but I believe it is very important. If a doctor always attempts to relate to the "strength" of a patient and his family, the patient and family will automatically respond out of their strength. When patients respond out of strength, they are automatically more of a resource to their own health. A patient or family may put its "weak side" forward when relating to a doctor, but this does not require that the doctor respond to that weak side.

An example of how people can become entangled in one another's weak sides is the following: A gets anxious and, as a consequence, pressures B to think, feel, or act in ways that will reduce A's anxiety. A is presenting his weak side to B, the side that pressures others to assume more responsibility for his own emotional well-being. If B reacts to A's anxiety by accommodating in an effort to make A less anxious (and, consequently, B less anxious), then B is allowing his weak side to respond to A's weak side. B opts for short-term relief at the expense of perpetuating a long-term problem. B may know better, but it is easier to give in and go along. B is always hopeful that someday *A will change* and, consequently, will "need" or demand less. In contrast, if B can operate based on his thinking rather than based on pressure from A, then B can relate to the "strong" or more mature side of A. This usually means not treating A like a child, one who must have others accommodate for him to feel better. In contrast to treating A like a child, B treats A as a person who can think for himself, as one who can draw on internal resources. If B relates to A out of B's "strength," A will respond out of "strength." This is a simple model, but, in many ways, it is that simple.

Many "levels" of doctor-patient relationship exist, ranging from very mature to very immature levels. A cardinal principle for conducting psychotherapy is to always assume that any immature aspects of a patient's dealings with his therapist that are persistent are somehow fostered or supported by immaturity that exists in the therapist. It is easy to blame a patient for the therapist's problems, but it is, obviously, impossible to conduct successful therapy with such an attitude. This is why so much of the training of therapists focuses on the therapist's recognizing and managing his own immaturity. A therapist or doctor can get anxiously focused on perceived weaknesses in a patient in the same way a parent can get anxiously focused on perceived weaknesses in a child. The more these weaknesses are focused on, the more exaggerated they become. In a family, problems escalate when family members lose sight of their own part in creating the problems that exist and, as a consequence, focus on getting one another to be different. The same process can occur in a medical setting. However, if doctors, nurses, and other medical staff always attempt to focus on their own attitudes and anxieties, always being alert for the patient's behavior being a reflection of their own, the patient is much less likely to become a repository for the medical system's anxiety and much less likely to become a victim of the system's sometimes rigidly held beliefs about what is "good for people."

CONCLUSION

Systems thinking has a tremendous potential in medicine and will ultimately form, I believe, the basis for an integrative theory. Much of the compartmentalization that presently exists in medicine should eventually disappear. Treatment subspecialties and their associated expertise will always exist, but a comprehensive theory about physical and emotional functioning and behavior can reduce much of the compartmentalization in medicine. If medicine can become less symptom-focused, more able to view the symptom within the larger context of the individual and to view the individual within the larger context of his important relationship systems, it will make symptoms more manageable for those who have them.

REFERENCES

Hinkle, L. E. and H. G. Wolff. 1957. "Health and the Social Environment: Experimental Investigation." In: *Explorations in Social Psychiatry*. A. H. Leighton, J. A. Clausen, and R. N. Wilson, eds. New York: Basic Books Inc.

Hinkle, L. E. 1959. "Physical Health, Mental Health and the Social Environment: Some Characteristics of Healthy and Unhealthy People." In: *Recent Contributions of Biological Psychological Investigations to Preventive Psychiatry*. Proceedings of the 2nd Institute on Preventive Psychiatry, University of Iowa, 1959. R. H. Ojemann, ed. Ames, Iowa: Iowa State University Press.

ON EMOTIONAL PROCESS IN SOCIETY

MURRAY BOWEN, MD

This is a report about the least understood concept in my family systems theory. Few things in life have provided more personal satisfaction than the discovery of a logical conceptual bridge between emotional process in the family and emotional process in society. I had worked on this as a background project for over fifteen years. We had detailed knowledge about the family. Many of the same patterns also operated in society. The answer seemed so obvious that anyone could know it, but it was so elusive it could evade discovery for decades. Awareness came suddenly while writing a paper late in 1972 and early in 1973. It was a minor version of finding a "missing link." Time has not permitted writing a paper in sufficient detail for the concept to be understandable to any but the most serious students. This will be a report *about* the concept.

All my life I have been interested in explanations for societal and international events. At any one time in history writers have pronounced society to be in the most decadent state since the beginning of time and have predicted doomsday as just around the corner. In the same periods others have predicted the glories of future civilizations. There has never been an explanation for war that goes far beyond the usual cause and effect thinking. On a more serious level there have been the analyses of historians, philosophers, and political and social scientists. Most of these have used logical deductive reasoning that explained events in retrospect. There are a few fascinating predictions of the future that appear to have been based more on intuition than known fact.

Published in Volume 1, No. 3, Summer 1979.

When I came into psychiatry I was delighted with a different order of reasoning that might provide better answers. Then I discovered that psychoanalysts tended to make sweeping generalizations from specific knowledge about the individual. For instance, there were generalizations that societies went through the same stages of psychosexual development as the individual. Perhaps the best explanations were the Jungian concepts such as a group unconscious. The average psychiatric explanation made the error of applying the psychology of the individual to society as a whole.

The family research of the 1950s added a completely new dimension to theoretical thinking. For the first time it was possible to view the family, rather than the individual, as a single emotional-psychological unit. Most family researchers and family therapists continued, to some degree, to see the family as a collection of individuals, and to see emotional "stuck togetherness" as a pathological state. There is an accuracy to this individual view but it misses the emotional bonding, of varying intensity, that welds all families into a unit. This beginning new view of the family as a unit quickly led some therapists toward superficial comparisons between the family and social groups.

There were numerous early efforts to extend family thinking to work and social groups. Emotional process in a family is similar to emotional process among people who work together. Early family therapists were quick to assume that work and social groups *were* families. This practice is still so prevalent that many accept it as fact. However much the relationships at work are similar to relationships in the family, there are important differences that are missed when people talk and function as if they are the same. I was supersensitive to false analogies. In my NIMH research I went along for a time with the notion the ward staff *was* a family. By 1956, we were following a strict interpretation of "family" in the research which helped to focus on the differences between relationships in families and in work and social systems.

Then came the concept of the triangle. The triangle is the molecule of any emotional system. It operates between any three people who come together for a task. I had hoped the triangle would eventually become the bridge to understand the specific connection between emotional process in the family and larger groups of people. This never evolved. Knowledge about triangles provided an important dimension but it was not the key to the puzzle. I was sure that somewhere in this increasing body of knowledge about families there was a logical conceptual bridge that would lead to a more precise understanding of emotional process in society. During the 1960s I avoided quick analogies and premature speculations and devoted myself to keeping files and bibliographies from the literature, pertinent clinical data, and writings from newspapers and magazines that seemed to highlight the process. In the meantime the "family" profession continued to use loose analogies and make inaccurate comparisons between family process and societal process. For me, the societal issue became a huge puzzle that was always in the background awaiting some new bit of evidence.

The next chapter evolved in 1972 when Anton Schmalz asked me to prepare a paper for a meeting of the Environmental Protection Agency. He was bringing together a broad spectrum of scientists to meet with important government figures. The scientists were researchers in population explosion, pollution, energy problems, the dwindling food supply, waste disposal, and alternative solutions to environmental problems. He asked me to address the predictable human reactions to environmental crisis. I began the task expecting to describe an assortment of human reactions as man damaged and then attempted to repair the damage to his environment. I had fifteen years of experience observing families as some dealt responsibly with the environment and as others devastated the environment for their personal gain.

The writing of that paper was one of the most satisfying and grueling experiences in my life. There were unanswered questions for which I returned to my files of substantiating data. In the midst of that complex and chaotic process I was finally able to see a logical theoretical bridge between emotional process in the family and emotional process in society. I was elated at the discovery, but time demands for the EPA meeting made it impossible to write about all the details. The paper became an abstraction of theory, a condensation of clinical data, and an explanation of conclusions. It satisfied the EPA but involved too many leaps in theory to satisfy others except those knowledgeable in family systems theory. The important part is that I knew I was on target and that the concept of *societal regression* was as solid as the other concepts in my theory.

In 1974 I introduced the concept of *emotional process in society* or *societal regression* as one of the eight concepts in the total family systems theory. Some family researchers reacted emotionally as if I had become the victim of some unrealistic thinking process. In 1974-75 I attempted to write about the societal issue in detail, but it became a book length production at a time when other family areas needed more attention. The result is that the concept has been presented as an extended outline but not in sufficient detail for those not familiar with family systems theory.

There are several important variables in the bridge between family and societal process. Each variable is based on theoretical concepts that have been described in published papers. The most important is the level of *differentiation of self*. Well differentiated families adapt well in any kind of stress. Poorly differentiated families collapse into dysfunction in minor stress. Most of us are on a continuum from poorly differentiated to well differentiated families.

Each general level of differentiation has a clearly defined life style for which that family is programmed.

Life style is determined by mechanisms for adapting to anxiety. The key variable that led to the discovery of the "bridge" was delinquency or an antisocial symptom in the family. The life style that led to the symptom had been present in the family for many years. From the life style in the family, and from the intensity and type of the symptom, it was possible to establish a fairly accurate functional level of differentiation by estimating the total family rather than the individual. It is possible for the same symptom to erupt in extremely rigid families or in more flexible families with better functional levels of differentiation. When antisocial symptoms erupt, they come within the province of societal agencies. The schools, police, probation officers, social agencies, juvenile judges, and other higher societal authorities become involved in the process. It is possible to establish a fairly accurate functional level of differentiation for each agency involved in the problem. It is often easy to establish these functional levels from the life styles, social attitudes, and mechanisms for dealing with anxiety of those who establish policy in the agencies. From my study of records from the late 1950s to 1972, the average functional level of differentiation in the societal agencies had dropped markedly. The operating policies of the agencies is determined by societal pressure. The interpretation of these findings is in other papers. The important factor is the bridge between family and societal process in the delinquent person whose problem develops in his family and who then becomes the responsibility of society.

Another important variable in this concept is the *level of anxiety*. For the purpose of this study, anxiety was defined as emotional reactiveness of the organism to real or imagined stress. The level of anxiety is intergeared with the functional level of differentiation of self. From a very broad viewpoint, the higher the level of anxiety, the lower the level of *functional* differentiation.

There are families with marginal levels of differentiation that appear to be "normal" when anxiety is low and that develop symptoms and become dysfunctional when the level of anxiety increases. When anxiety decreases, the reverse cycle takes place. Since the early 1960s the United States has been in an increasing level of anxiety with only brief periods of decreasing anxiety. This pattern has not been remarkably different from worldwide anxiety.

Another variable is the togetherness-individuality balance of emotional forces. This provides microscopic evidence for tracking the background process in families or in society. As anxiety mounts, the human organism makes automatic moves toward togetherness which is never achieved. This huddling together creates new anxiety, which results in more emotional distance, which results in more panicky striving for closeness, which results in more distance. When anxiety decreases, the striving for emotional closeness decreases and there is more emphasis on the responsibility of the individual. The rights-responsibility issue provides another background index of the process. When anxiety increases there is a focus on the rights of the individual and less emphasis on the responsibility of the individual which guarantees those rights. When anxiety decreases there is a rising focus on responsibility and individuality and less focus on togetherness and rights. The rights-responsibility issue even influences decisions made by the Supreme Court.

From the studies of the 1972–73 period, it was clear to me that we have been in a massive regression that began in the mid–1960s. There have been only brief periods of calm followed by brief periods of "progression." The regressive pattern is identical to that in regressing families on their way to psychosis and functional collapse. When symptoms develop there is no motivation to change the life style that gave rise to the symptoms. Instead the effort goes toward momentary symptom relief which leads ultimately to a deeper step into the regression. The same pattern applies to national efforts to repair social problems. When anxiety is high, the legislation predictably goes to "band-aid" measures to relieve the anxiety of the moment. In 1973–74, I wrote about this process as "societal regression" which since then I have tried to present as one phase of a process that also includes societal progression.

These variables are based on observable, knowable, and predictable facts that apply to families and larger social systems. In addition to the knowable facts, there are assumptions about factors that increase or decrease societal anxiety. From some twenty years experience considering the dozens of factors that others have mentioned, and that could stimulate such sustained anxiety, it is my working assumption that the anxiety is related to population explosion and the rapid depletion of the earth's raw materials that threaten continuation of life on the planet in the style to which the human has been accustomed. The predictions made in 1973 were based on the predictable way families and small social groups handle sustained anxiety. The biological being that is the human cannot change his life style in a short time. If the assumptions about societal anxiety are reasonably accurate, there will be no more than brief decreases in anxiety in the coming generations. The sequence of events suggests that the human horde will follow the predictable course of biological organisms under stress, relatively uninfluenced by intellectual reasoning. The rapid evolution of events since 1973 has provided firmer evidence that the assumptions are in the right ballpark.

There are numerous factors in the societal concepts for which more substantiation is needed. I would like more time to work on these details. With inflation and energy problems increasing, and with other equally pressing problems in the wings waiting for a place on stage, there is evidence that society is far calmer now than it will be five or ten years into the future.

STRESS, SOCIETY, AND THE INDIVIDUAL

DANIEL V. PAPERO, PhD, MSSW

While in training many years ago I did a field placement in the school social work service of the Nashville, Tennessee public schools. Currently I find myself once again extraordinarily interested in the public school system, and that interest has led me to a small project with selected schools in a neighboring community.

I believe that two great processes underlie all current large scale social change—increasing population and decreasing resources. Even if resources prove to be adequate, they are unevenly distributed across the globe.

These two processes combine to produce great dislocation of population, a process already underway and one that appears likely to accelerate in the foreseeable future. If research models of population density in animals hold true, the population shifts will not occur with people spreading themselves out across available space. Rather, huge numbers of people will congregate in relatively small spaces with large tracts of underpopulated surrounding areas.

Recent federal government projections predict that the population in the United States for the next decade is to increase by a third, roughly an increase of 100 million people. Fifty percent of that growth is projected to occur in California. Another thirty-five to forty percent is projected for the East Coast from Tidewater Virginia to Boston and in South Florida. The remainder will be spread along the cities of the Gulf Coast. The vast interior

Published in Volume 17, No. 1, Fall 1996.

This is an edited version of a presentation made to the Fairfax Association of School Social Workers and Visiting Teachers on March 27, 1996.

portions of the United States will experience much less growth and may even decline in population. The animal models seem to be predictive.

Even though the logistical management (provisions of food and sanitation) of such huge, dense populations will be a monumental challenge, I believe it is within the human capacity to resolve that challenge.

The more significant challenge, as I see it, is to the human capacity to develop and maintain the complex behaviors of self management and the skills of maintaining a relationship network. The animal models suggest that as population density increases, physiological processes of stress lead to the breakdown of complex reciprocal behaviors and the emergence of highly reactive, self-centered behaviors. While these behaviors may achieve short-term gain for those individuals engaged in them, the overall deterioration of the social climate ultimately spells death for the animal populations.

The human population is no more immune to the physiological processes of stress connected to population density than are the animal models. While the subject of the physiological stress response, fascinating in its own right, is far too broad to go into tonight, let me mention briefly the psychology of stress and its effects on individual and group functioning.

Four general psychological variables modulate and intensify the physiology of stress. The first is control. When an individual believes he or she has some control over the stressor and the stressful situation, the intensity of the physiological stress response is much lessened. The operational word is "believe," for research has indicated that one need not have actual control of the situation as long as one believes one has that control.

The second is predictability. When a stressor is predictable, the individual experiences a less severe stress response than when unpredictability reigns. Research has even demonstrated that disruption of predictability is itself a stressor.

The third concerns the availability and effectiveness of anxiety-binding mechanisms or outlets for frustration. With the availability of such mechanisms, the impact of physiological stress is decreased.

The fourth concerns perception or how people are looking at the world. When people perceive a situation as worsening, the impact of stress is intensified. Whether one sees the glass as half empty or half full really is important.

Stress affects the individual in predictable ways. He or she becomes more sensitive, mental flexibility decreases, and automatic, reactive behavior directed toward relief of discomfort increases.

Status interactions become increasingly important. Who defers to whom and who is ahead of whom are monitored with exquisite sensitivity. The automatic behaviors reflecting the reactivity to perceived status shifts play out in unmistakable fashion: attack, defend, pursue and withdraw.

Stress is, as everyone knows, highly contagious, and as it races through a group, large numbers of people become more sensitive, less thoughtful, and more self-centeredly reactive.

One can speak accurately of a storm of stress as anxiety moves through a group. There are predictable markers that both reflect the movement of the storm and express its intensity.

One of the earliest harbingers is the accelerating use of anxiety-binding mechanisms to meet the rising tide of stress. Substance abuse, displacement behaviors of various kinds, sexually focused activities, and general avoidance of perceived sources of stress become more prominent. The anxiety binding mechanisms themselves, when overused, generate further stress in a potentially vicious spiral.

Another early marker is the disruption of relationships. Relationships that in less turbulent times can be maintained and are workable no longer remain so. Coalitions form and dissipate with increasing rapidity as stress spreads and intensifies. Conflicts erupt and intensify. As more and more people are drawn into the spiral, intense polarizations marked by accelerating and intensifying competition begin to divide the group into highly sensitized, narrowly focused, and highly reactive segments determined to maintain their position at all costs. Versions of the Hatfields and McCoys appear in almost every conceivable arena.

Group membership and short-term competitive advantage drive the decision-making processes. Greater and greater numbers of people lose their ability to see a bigger picture and manage themselves responsibly. In such a climate, the concept of individual rights becomes increasingly irrelevant as highly reactive groups press for their rights while the stable social infrastructure required to maintain an operational code of rights erodes.

The ability of people to maintain cooperative relationships begins to break down at all levels. Parents begin to be less sure of themselves, more anxious about their children, and more reactive to one another. Teachers and parents become adversaries, even though each shares the same intense interest in the welfare of the child. Neighbors resort to threats and suits to handle relatively trivial matters. People begin to look toward identified and sometimes self-proclaimed leaders to solve problems that are far beyond the ability of any one individual to solve and are rooted in how people themselves are behaving. Terribly complex problems are approached simplistically, usually leading to a worsening of the problems. The great American researcher on the effects of population density, John B. Calhoun, talks about a process he refers to as *universal autism*,[1] the inability of individuals to respond appropriately to one another. Populations under such circumstances become highly unstable, driving the stress responses of individuals toward greater intensity.

---

[1] See p. 33, *Universal Autism: Extinction Resulting from Failure to Develop Relationships.*

I don't pretend to know whether such scenarios of universal autism on a grand scale will ever occur. I believe one can observe such processes and markers at work on a small scale in communities across the world.

The effects of population migration have already reached the Washington area. According to Fairfax County statistics, county population increased thirty-seven percent between 1980 and 1990, a gain in numbers of 261,266 people. By 2005, county population is projected to increase to more than a million residents. And already some of the markers of the storm of stress and anxiety have appeared.

The stress research literature and the study of human family emotional processes provide some clues as to what may be required of individuals if the projected storms of stress and social disruption are to be contained and to some degree weathered. The MacArthur prize-winning neuroscientist and stress researcher, Robert M. Sapolsky,[2] has identified a class of animals that show the lowest levels of stress, have the best health, and live the longest of any. They also function toward the top of the hierarchy of animals. Animals of this class display the following five characteristics that may serve as at least a partial list of the characteristics that individuals and leaders will have to develop and employ in the stressful societies of the present and the future: (1) They excel at threat discrimination; that is, they are very good at knowing what constitutes a real threat and what does not. (2) When they have noted a threat, they typically initiate the response. Since they almost always prevail in such interactions, Sapolsky believes that they possess broad and refined knowledge of the network of relationships and that they pick their battles wisely. (3) They are very clear about whether they have won or lost an encounter and

---

[2] Robert M. Sapolsky. 1992. *Stress, the Aging Brain, and Mechanisms of Neuron Death.* Cambridge, Massachusetts: The MIT Press.

they accept the outcome immediately. (4) They displace frustration effectively. (5) They maintain a broad network of relationships within the group. Sapolsky describes them as simply having a large network of friends. This latter skill, the ability to maintain a broad network of relationships, Sapolsky believes, may be the most critical of all. It is, if the animal models are to be believed, the ability that is most severely influenced by stress.

Self-management lies at the heart of relationship maintenance. Humans have always known about the importance of self-management. Religious texts pulse with the injunctions to manage self. The management literature extols its virtues. In its most basic form, self-management has to do with the individual's ability to recognize, tolerate and ultimately manage the gut wrenching discomfort of one's own fear. And the ultimate challenge to self-management occurs when one is in direct contact with the emotional reactivity of an anxious other. It requires managing one's own reactivity and tolerating the reactivity of others.

Self-management is not a passive activity. It requires knowledge of self and the expression of self in action. It demands that an individual recognize and regulate his or her own sensitivity to others, that he or she develop mechanisms to expand mental flexibility and acuity under the pressures that tend to decrease that very flexibility and acuity, and that he or she act on the basis of thought and knowledge in the situations that promote emotionally reactive behavior. Small challenge!

Self-management addresses the four psychological variables associated with physiological stress. Control and predictability begin with oneself. Controlling one's own behavior and predicting one's own emotional reactivity form the foundation for a sense of control and predictability in broader arenas.

Self-management requires that a person develop and employ mechanisms to help regulate stress and anxiety. And perhaps most importantly, self-management requires that a person begin to understand and manage his or her own perception of events. This may be the most difficult arena of all.

The management of one's own perceptual processes assumes that a person has developed a few simple skills. I will mention a few of them briefly. The first skill is the awareness that one's own perception of a situation is not a fully accurate rendition of that situation. We all see what we have been trained and expect to see. Consequently we miss things right in front of our eyes. For example, we are trained to see and think of pathology, and consequently we find it. In the process, we often miss the strength of people and of their actions.

The second skill involves the effort to see a few of the things to which we have been perceptually blind. This involves challenging our own deeply held notions of how the world works, subjecting our notions to the test of what is and what can be observed. Often the obvious things are the most important, yet we discard them because they are obvious. For example, we know that one emotionally reactive and upset person can be aided by another who does nothing more than stay in contact and remain calmer than the upset other. Any parent who has dealt with an upset child knows that how he or she handles anxiety is directly linked to whether the child is able to manage upset or not.

Another important skill deals with knowledge of how our relationships influence our perception of events. Emotionally charged contact with another can shift the way we see events, not on the basis of our own observations and our efforts to find facts but because the contact has increased our own stress and anxiety, automatically shifting the psychological filters through which we apprehend the world.

Self-management becomes an important component of leadership, a function that is likely to be extremely important to society in the future. While designated leadership roles will be important, probably informal leadership will be more important.

What we know from the world of the human family is that family functioning begins to change when a leader emerges in the family. Some of the characteristics of such a family leader may also shed some light on what may be required of leaders in our future. Murray Bowen wrote of leadership in the family in the following way:

> Operationally, ideal family treatment begins when one can find a family leader with the courage to define self, who is as invested in the welfare of the family as in self, who is neither angry nor dogmatic, whose energy goes to changing self rather than telling others what they should do, who can know and respect the multiple opinions of others, who can modify self in response to the strengths of the group, and who is not influenced by the irresponsible opinions of others. . . . A family leader is beyond the popular notion of power. A responsible family leader automatically generates mature leadership qualities in other family members who are to follow. [3]

A leader will have to demonstrate these qualities and not just tell others about them. When people are stressed and emotionally reactive, they respond to who leaders are and what they do rather than what they say. But in the same sense that stress and anxiety are infectious, high level functioning under pressure is extremely attractive. An important task of leadership will be to find a way to lend a hand to stressed others to pick up their own functioning and to become a leader in the manner described in their own families, neighborhoods, and work groups.

The future of our society will be determined by the balance between such leadership and the highly reactive, stress-driven group processes of fragmentation, polarization, and conflict without its companion, reconciliation.

---

[3] Michael E. Kerr and Murray Bowen. 1988. *Family Evaluation.* New York: W. W. Norton & Company, pp. 342–343.

The following quotation is attributed to Albert Einstein and is taken out of his context, theoretical physics: "The significant problems we face cannot be solved at the same level of thinking we were at when we created them." Like the military that is always prepared to fight the last war, most of us gear our lives to handle in the future the problems we have encountered in the past. Like the military the problems of the present tend to be linked to those past solutions and catch us unprepared. We then tend to employ measures we have used in the past and, in unstable and stressful conditions, those measures have a likelihood of making the current problems worse.

Organizations are already changing to meet the requirements of a rapidly changing and uncertain future. Peter Senge, of the Sloan School of Business at MIT, writes about his vision of what organizations in the future will have to be. He writes of the "learning organization,"

> . . . organizations where people continually expand their capacity to create the results they truly desire, where new and expansive patterns of thinking are nurtured, where collective aspiration is set free, and where people are continually learning how to learn together.[4]

While it may sound ideal, Senge points to specific organizations that have been unusually successful at adapting to changing conditions with a minimum of disruption, using the fundamental skills of relationship maintenance and cooperative behavior to guide their activities.

One of the characteristics of these unusual organizations has been the ability to create flexible cooperative work groups that shift personnel as the environments shift. Job descriptions

---

[4] Peter M. Senge. 1990. *The Fifth Discipline: The Art and Practice of the Learning Organization.* New York: Doubleday Currency, p. 3.

become less important than the skills that the individual can bring to a particular task or endeavor. In a continuous process of learning and self-management, these organizations have found ways to manage the turf battles that can polarize and cripple an organization. Somehow, cooperative behavior has come to be seen as in everyone's self-interest.

Frances Fukuyama of the Rand Corporation writes about the concept of *social capital*, the fundamental infrastructure upon which major corporations and organizations are built. Social capital is the network of relationships that are built up over time that allow nongenetically related individuals to engage and cooperate with one another. While such networks take time to develop, they can erode rapidly.

Why do I come back to my preoccupation with cooperative behavior? Aside from my own idealism, I will return once more to the work of Jack Calhoun and his research on the effects of population density. Having seen experimentally how density led to physiological stress and the breakdown of complex behaviors, he wondered whether behaviors could be identified that helped his subjects maintain functioning under the increasing pressure of population density.

Calhoun trained a group of animals to cooperate with one another. He discovered that these animals could tolerate and function in levels of population density several times higher than untrained animals could. If the animal models are to be believed, cooperative behavior will be of considerable value in the times to come.

The public school will sit at the center of the social storm, even more so than it does now. No other public agency has such a wide-ranging connection to a broad community and to individual families over as long a period of time. Children and families of various ethnic and socioeconomic backgrounds and communities will contact one another in the schools. There will be tensions and opportunities. In many ways, as the schools go, so goes the community.

I believe that individual schools will have an enormous opportunity to play a major role in the stabilization of entire neighborhoods and even communities against the rising tide of stress-based erosion of complex functioning. The task, if it is to be accepted, will involve courageous, thoughtful leadership, not just of designated leaders but of individuals at all levels within the school organization.

That social work could be a part of that leadership goes without saying. So could psychology, psychiatry, and the National Education Association. Here Einstein's comment once again surfaces: "The significant problems we face cannot be solved at the same level of thinking we were at when we created them." Peter Senge writes of vision as one of the central challenges of leadership, a vision that extends beyond self.

The leader of a learning organization not only develops his or her own personal vision, he or she encourages others to do so as well. From personal visions a shared vision can develop. So important is the development of shared vision that Senge considers it the central element of the daily work of leaders. This involves designing and fostering the core ideas or beliefs that will guide the organization. The leader leads primarily by example, guided by systems thinking. The leader does not sell or require that others accept his or her vision. Rather they have free choice to participate in the shared vision and accept responsibility for making the vision a reality.

So the gauntlet has been thrown, the challenge waiting to be accepted. Einstein, Calhoun, Sapolsky and Senge have helped to define the dilemma. It is up to social work, psychology, psychiatry, and any other group, professional or otherwise, to lead the effort toward principled functioning, practiced under pressure, with an awareness of interdependence and the importance of cooperative activity.